CONTENTS

VOLUME 28
British History from the Restoration

Cover picture: The Royal Family, painted in 1846 by Franz Xavier Winterhalter. Queen Victoria (1819-1901) gave her name to an era epitomizing British imperialism. Her marriage to Prince Albert of Saxe-Coburg-Gotha (1819-1861) continued a system of intermarriage among the royal families of Europe that was to bind together countries in an informal diplomatic linking.

The Restoration of the Stuarts

The powers and position of the English monarchy, restored in 1660, were defined by the Convention Parliament (1660) and in the early sessions of the Cavalier Parliament (1661–79). Both these assemblies, like Charles II (1630–85) himself, wished to avoid the extremes of recent years. Parliament insisted on maintaining the limitations imposed on the Crown by the "constitutional revolution" of 1640–41. The king was not granted too large a revenue, so that he would be forced to call Parliament frequently to ask for more. Thus Charles had to summon Parliament almost every year until the very end of his reign. The gentry who sat in Charles II's parliaments were quite prepared to uphold the royal authority, provided the king used it in ways they approved.

The religious settlement

Charles's success as king therefore depended on his ability to keep the trust and goodwill of the House of Commons, above all by respecting the religious prejudices of the country. In the 1640s the old Church of England had been dismantled. In the resulting vacuum of religious authority new movements such as the Baptists and Quakers had grown and multiplied. The House of Commons of 1661, however, re-established the Church of England with severe laws against Protestant Nonconformists. Charles was not happy with this extremism. Apart from his personal Catholic tendencies, he was tolerant by nature. In 1660, before returning to England, he issued a declaration at Breda promising liberty to tender consciences, subject to the approval of Parliament. Parliament would not let him keep his promise, but Charles tried in 1662 and 1672 to procure greater liberty for Nonconformists.

More explosive was the problem of Catholicism, which became linked in the 1670s with questions of foreign policy. In 1670 Charles allied himself with Louis XIV (reigned 1643–1715) of France [Key]. In 1672 together they attacked the Protestant Dutch Republic, which was almost overrun by Louis's army. Louis was already feared as the archetype of absolutism and militant Catholicism, and Charles's alliance with him seemed doubly sinister when it became clear in the 1670s that Charles's brother James, Duke of York (1633–1701) [7], later James II, had become a Catholic. As Charles had no legitimate children, James was the heir apparent, and the prospect of the first Catholic monarch in England since Mary (reigned 1553–8) overshadowed the politics of the last half of Charles's reign.

Opposition to Catholicism

English Protestants had long identified Catholic rulers with both absolutism and cruel persecution [4]. In 1678 Titus Oates (1649–1705) [5], a disreputable adventurer, came forward with allegations of a "Popish Plot" to assassinate Charles and make James king. Three times between 1679 and 1681 the Commons passed bills to exclude the Duke of York from the succession, but neither the king nor the Lords would agree to them. Led by Anthony Ashley Cooper, Earl of Shaftesbury (1621–83) [6] the "Exclusionists" (who formed the nucleus of the embryonic Whig Party) mounted a strident campaign of petitions, propaganda and demonstrations. Echoes of the Civil War

CONNECTIONS

See also
Pepys's London
Scotland from 1560 to the Act of Union
The age of Marlborough

In other volumes
The English revolution (26)
The Commonwealth and Protectorate (26)
The age of Louis XIV (29)
Art and architecture in the 17th century (34)

1 The Treaty of Breda (1667) ended the 2nd Anglo-Dutch War. England thus renounced claims to the Dutch East Indies, but in return gained control of New York and New Jersey. Earlier, in 1660, Charles issued a declaration at Breda, in The Netherlands, promising a general pardon for activities during the revolution, as well as religious toleration, should he be invited back to the throne. He thus removed any obstacles to his restoration.

2 Charles II, unlike his father and brother, was a charming and popular man, although reluctant to devote himself to the details of government. Temperamentally suited to absolute government, he was determined not to be exiled again; and his cynical view of human nature made him try to control his ministers by playing one off against another. Much of the politics of his reign was therefore confused. This bust was made by Honore Pellé.

3 The Royal Society was incorporated by Charles II in 1662. At that time interest in science was fashionable. The Society's early proceedings ranged from demography to botany, reflecting the polymathic interests of the members. The early Fellows included courtiers and dilettantes as well as men of outstanding talent such as Wren, Boyle and Newton. Above all, perhaps, the Society spread an understanding of "natural philosophy" to the ruling élite of England and thus contributed to the acceptance of the social thought of the Enlightenment and indirectly inspired the Industrial Revolution.

4 Fear of Catholicism during the Restoration was based on the Protestant feeling that not only was it erroneous and idolatrous theologically, but that it was a malign political force as well. It was thought that Catholic rulers, however gentle by nature, would be forced by the pope to persecute Protestants. The aggressive rule of Louis XIV in France seemed to show a clear link between Catholicism and absolutism, attacking Protestants both in his own kingdom and in the Dutch Republic. In particular the Revocation of the Edict of Nantes by Louis XIV in 1685 ended all toleration of Protestants in France. Many went into exile in England and their reports of Catholic intolerance added weight to the Protestants' fears of James II. Thus when James imprisoned for sedition seven bishops who refused to read his Declaration of Indulgence in May 1688 that promised toleration to the Catholics, as well as Dissenters, his attack on the Anglican Church, was seen as an attack on the rule of law.

agitations worried the more conservative opponents of Exclusion (who became known as Tories). They rallied to the king and helped Charles survive the exclusion crisis, permitting the peaceful accession of James II in 1685.

At first all went smoothly. James easily crushed a rebellion by James, Duke of Monmouth (1649–85) [8], an illegitimate son of Charles II and James's Protestant rival for the throne in the Exclusion crisis. But the Tories' co-operation with James soon ended. James hoped to give the Catholics religious liberty and political equality by repealing all the laws that prohibited Catholic worship and excluded Catholics from public office. The Tory Parliament of 1685 was strongly royalist but also strongly anti-Catholic. Annoyed by the Tories' hostility, James tried to persuade the Protestant dissenters to support a general toleration that would include Catholics. In 1686, despite opposition from Archbishop Sancroft (1617–93), he set up an ecclesiastic commission that was seen as an attempt to subject the Church to his religious policies. Meanwhile he stretched his powers as Charles I had done in order to admit Catholics to places in the army, the administration and the universities.

The "Glorious Revolution"

James's nephew, William III of Orange (1650–1702), was closely interested in developments in England. Already the dominant political figure in the Dutch Republic, William had a claim to the English throne through his wife Mary, James's elder daughter, and he was eager to use England's fleet and wealth in his lifelong struggle against France. By 1688 William feared that he might be cheated of the succession, because late in 1687 it was announced that James's queen was pregnant. By the time James's son was born, in June 1688, William had decided to invade England in response to an invitation from leading political figures. He landed with his army on 5 November [9]. James fled to France and in February 1689 Parliament offered the crown jointly to William and Mary, and the rule of law, enshrining the supremacy of the landed interest over the monarch, was assured.

Charles II usually followed Louis XIV, not vice versa as in this cartoon. Except for the period 1678–81, Charles was allied with Louis (whose power he envied) or was benevolently neutral. Louis gave him several subsidies to help him to stay independent at home, and to resist Parliament's demands for a war against Louis, whom most Englishmen saw as the main enemy. Initially Charles sought the French alliance to avenge England's failure to win the 2nd Anglo-Dutch War of 1665–7.

5 Titus Oates, the main witness in the Popish Plot, had spent a year as a Jesuit novice and the stories that he told were based on the information he collected at various seminaries. Despite inconsistencies, he spoke so compellingly that many believed him. The murder of the magistrate to whom Oates first recounted the plot appeared to confirm all that he said. In 1685, however, he was convicted of perjury and flogged. The crisis allowed Shaftesbury, a former supporter of Charles who now feared his conversion to Roman Catholicism, to drum up anti-Catholic agitation and turn it against James, the Catholic heir to the throne. He died in voluntary exile in Holland.

5

6

6 The Earl of Shaftesbury had been a royal minister in the 1660s and early 1670s. His organization of the Exclusionists into a coherent parliamentary group was important for the development of political parties.

7

7 James II served as an able commander of the fleet during the 2nd Anglo-Dutch War, but as a Catholic he lacked Charles's popularity, and quickly alienated all the support that he had at his accession.

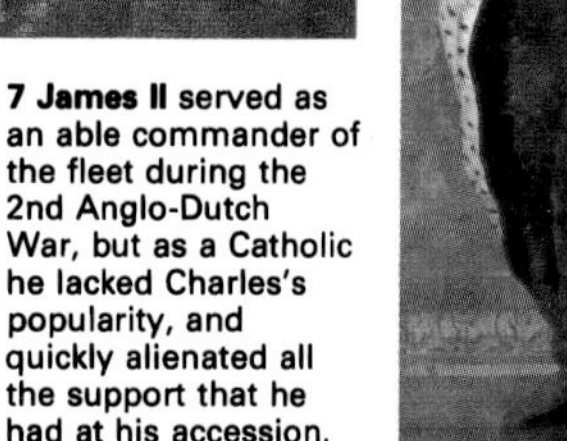

8

8 The Duke of Monmouth landed in Dorset in 1685 to assert his claim to the throne. He won little gentry support and was easily beaten at Sedgemoor. His followers were treated with severity by Judge Jeffreys (*c.* 1648–89) in the so-called Bloody Assizes, at which 200 were hanged and 800 transported. Monmouth himself was executed.

9

9 William of Orange landed at Brixham late in 1688 with an army of 15,000 men. But his invasion succeeded without bloodshed (hence its name, the "Glorious Revolution"), as James's army commander John Churchill (1650–1722), later Duke of Marlborough, went over to William's side at the last moment, removing James's last source of support in the country.

Pepys's London

The London of Samuel Pepys (1633–1703) [Key] was small (Marylebone and Mile End were in the country) and consisted of two cities: London, the commercial and financial centre; and Westminster, centre of government, politics and aristocratic society. The two were so different, culturally and politically, that there was often tension between them. Pepys, however, straddled both worlds. A Londoner by birth and a civil servant by profession, he moved easily between his office and lodgings near the Tower and the court at Whitehall. A man of quick intelligence, who paid careful attention to detail, he rose from a comparatively menial post to become James II's chief naval administrator.

Diary of a somebody

There was nothing very unusual about Pepys's rise to wealth and prominence. The Tudor and Stuart civil service offered a career open to talents. What was unusual about Pepys was his diary, which gives an unequalled panorama of life in London between 1660 and 1669: the politics of court and Parliament; meetings with naval contractors and mistresses; music and the theatre; food and drink; and tensions at the office and quarrels with the neighbours.

Insatiably curious and endlessly sociable, Pepys wanted to know everything that was going on and jotted it down, in shorthand, when he got home. On 25 March 1661 he told how, returning home, he "took up a boy that had a lanthorn, that was picking up rags, and got him to light me home, and had great discourse with him, how he could get sometimes three or four bushells of rags in a day, and got 3d a bushell for them, and many other discourses, what and how many ways there are for poor children to get their livings honestly". Gossip about Charles II's sexual cavortings is juxtaposed with details of Admiralty business or the latest experiment performed before the Royal Society. National humiliations such as the Medway disaster [6] appear alongside details of a meal.

Congestion, crime and natural disasters

At the Restoration, London [1] was the largest city in England. Its population – not far short of 500,000 – was more than ten times that of Bristol, its nearest rival. Little more than a century earlier, its population had been only 50,000 and it now displayed all the symptoms of unplanned urban growth. Within the old medieval walls rising population and property values encouraged landlords to build upwards and to overcrowd their property [3] despite municipal attempts to control them.

The fastest growth was to the east and north – Stepney, Whitechapel, Shoreditch, Clerkenwell – and south of the river in Southwark. There the speculative builder and slum landlord operated almost unchecked. Jerrybuilt tenements and insanitary courts housed artisans and porters, watermen and sailors, Huguenots and Irish.

As the population had far outgrown the flimsy machinery of law and order, crime flourished. Violence was never far below the surface in Restoration London. Drunken quarrels ended in murder. Courtiers and soldiers showed a casual disregard for human life. On public holidays law students from the Inns of Court and gangs of apprentices roamed the streets looking for trouble.

CONNECTIONS

See also
The Restoration of the Stuarts
The age of Marlborough

In other volumes
Science and technology 1500-1700 (29)
Art and architecture in the 17th century (34)

1 London before the Great Fire was a chaotic jumble of houses. Old St Paul's dominated the skyline and London Bridge, lined with homes and shops, was the only bridge across the Thames. The city's streets, filthy with rubbish, were dangerous at night because of criminals. The River Thames served as the main highway. It was quicker and cleaner than the narrow and congested cobblestoned streets.

2 Charles II and his mistress Nell Gwynn converse in the presence of diarist John Evelyn (1620–1706). Such a scene, wrote Evelyn, made him "heartily sorry". He was shocked by the king's promiscuity.

3 Houses huddled against each other in London. Most dwellings were built of wood, (despite regulations against its use) and they had narrow frontages, steep roofs and projecting upper floors.

4 The plague of 1665–6 was carried by the rats that infested London's teeming tenements, and deaths exceeded 15 per cent of the population. By far the worst year was 1665. Carts trundled through the streets at night to collect corpses for communal burial. The court moved out of London as did many people. Houses touched by pestilence were vacated and the door marked with a red cross and with the words "Lord have mercy upon us".

Such a crowded, ill-housed population was vulnerable to the ravages of disease and fire, both of which struck terribly in the 1660s. The last great outbreak of bubonic plague (1665–6) [4] claimed more than 70,000 victims in London. Pepys wrote on 30 July 1665: "It was a sad noise to hear our bell to toll and ring so often to-day, either for deaths or burials; I think five or six times." The Great Fire of 1666 [5] destroyed most of the City of London. On 2 September Pepys watched the progress of the fire, "a most horrid malicious bloody flame".

Rebuilding and expansion

Out of this catastrophe came a chance to rebuild according to a single coherent plan [7] a great swathe of central London from the river up to London Wall and from Fenchurch Street to Fleet Street. From the ashes emerged a new city with broader, cleaner streets, brick-built houses, a much purer water supply and a whole series of churches [8] designed by the brilliant young architect Christopher Wren (1632–1723).

London had long been the greatest port in the kingdom, and under Charles II new trading companies were established, notably the Royal African and Hudson's Bay companies. But the main source of the impressive commercial growth of the 1670s and 1680s lay elsewhere. First, by protective legislation and naval power England began to challenge the Dutch dominance of the international carrying trade. This would at length enable London to replace Amsterdam as "the world's entrepôt". Second, these years saw a massive increase in imports and re-exports of sugar and tobacco from England's Caribbean and North American colonies. In addition, London was the hub of the growing internal trade within England.

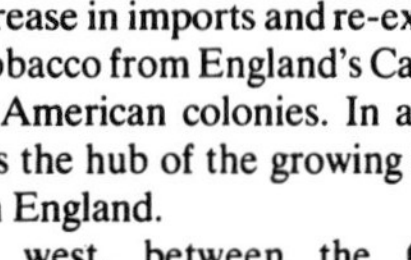

Farther west, between the City of London and the City of Westminster, lay an area that had largely escaped the fire. Here were the palaces of the nobility, situated within convenient distance of Parliament and the royal palaces of Whitehall and St James's. The Strand had been developed much earlier and the main growth areas in Pepys's day were in Pall Mall, Piccadilly and St Giles's Fields – around the West End of the future.

Samuel Pepys held an important post in the Navy Office, and was an MP and president of the Royal Society. His diary shows him to have been cultivated, fastidious, ambitious and lecherous.

5

5 The Great Fire (1666) began in a baker's house in Pudding Lane and raged for three days. It destroyed 13,000 houses, St Paul's, 87 parish churches and many public buildings. Deaths were few but half the population was rendered homeless.

6

6 A Dutch fleet sailed up the Medway in June 1667, found defences almost non-existent, and burned, sank or captured several of the king's greatest ships. The flagship *Royal Charles* was among those captured. Meanwhile, wrote Pepys bitterly, the king was chasing a moth with his mistress. The Dutch Wars flared intermittently from 1652 to 1674.

7

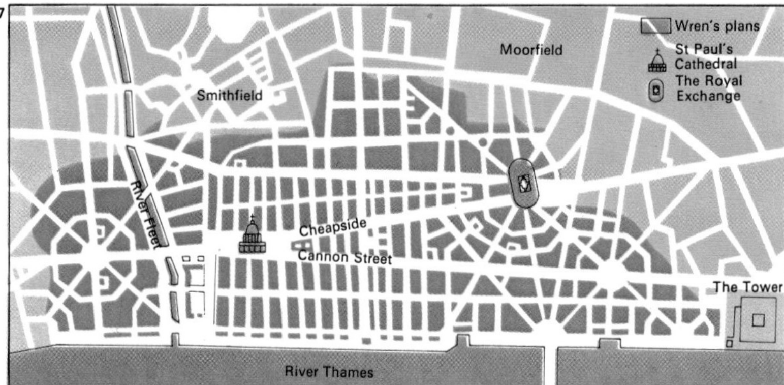

7 Several plans for rebuilding London were advanced after the Great Fire. Christopher Wren proposed that broad, straight streets should be laid down in a geometric pattern. A new St Paul's and Royal Exchange were the main focal points of his scheme, which featured several piazzas. But a shortage of money and conflicting interests meant that no scheme was adopted in full. Instead, the shape of the city was decided by a special committee.

8

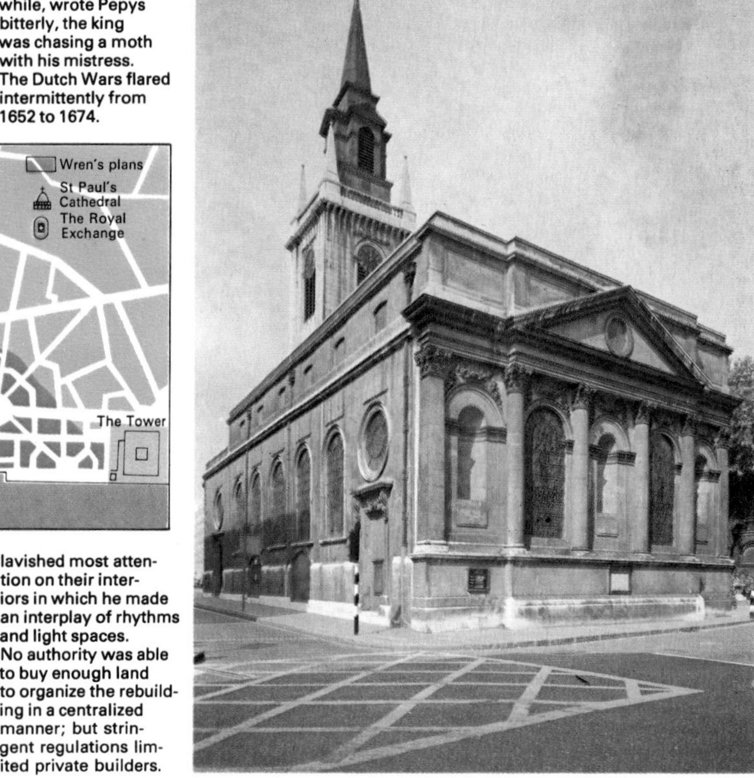

8 St Lawrence, Jewry, was one of the 53 churches that Christopher Wren built in London following the Great Fire. He was appointed Surveyor-General in 1669 with the task of rebuilding the city. These churches have distinctive spires but Wren lavished most attention on their interiors in which he made an interplay of rhythms and light spaces. No authority was able to buy enough land to organize the rebuilding in a centralized manner; but stringent regulations limited private builders.

Scotland from 1560 to the Act of Union

The religious upheavals in Scotland during the first half of the sixteenth century, initiated by the Reformation, found wide support for political as well as spiritual reasons. The new religious ideas were welcomed by those wishing to loosen the alliance with Catholic France in favour of England, and the nobles, who hoped to gain much from a weakening of the Church's power.

The Reformation and the Crown

With the abolition of papal authority in 1560, Calvinism quickly became the official belief in Scotland, but the ruler, Mary, Queen of Scots (reigned 1542–67), was a Catholic and a member of the French royal family [1]. On the death of her husband Francis II of France (reigned 1559–60), Mary returned to Scotland to try to establish her authority as queen.

She proved to be a clever politician but her power and public appeal were always limited by the tremendous influence of John Knox (1505–72), the leading preacher of the new church [3]. Eventually, in 1567, she was forced to abdicate by the nobility, who were angered at her turbulent marriages [2]. In 1568 she had to take refuge in England, and the nobles put her infant son James VI (reigned 1567–1625) on the Scottish throne with the expectation that a king so created would be their puppet.

On this point the nobles failed. James grew up to become the most effective ruler of any of the Stewarts. He did this without funds or force, but purely by negotiation and hard work, particularly helped by the fact that he was expected to inherit the English throne. He and his cousin, Elizabeth I of England (reigned 1558–1603), both wanted peace on the Border. In 1603, Elizabeth on her deathbed acknowledged James as her heir. James, known thereafter as James I, moved to England but continued to control Scotland as he said "by my pen" [Key].

James's son Charles I (reigned 1625–49) could not do this because he did not have the intimate knowledge of the country. His policy of personal rule made the Scottish nobility uneasy for their rights and powers while his religious policy was seen, rightly or wrongly, as contrary to Presbyterian principles. When Charles produced a prayer book for Scotland in 1637 [4] it provoked the Scots to formulate a claim for their traditional liberties – the National Covenant. Charles's attempts to bring an English army to suppress the Covenanters led to the Long Parliament, and thus contributed to the start of the English Civil War in 1642.

The English Parliament persuaded the Scots to join in the first Civil War (1642–6) by accepting the terms laid down by the Scots in the Solemn League and Covenant, of 1643. But after the war, power lay in the hands of the Parliamentarians' army, which wanted an independent church system with liberty for the individual congregation. Efforts by the Scots to insist on Presbyterianism led to the second Civil War (1648), the execution of Charles (1649) and occupation of Scotland by Oliver Cromwell (1599–1658) [6].

Stuart restoration and dethronement

When the English Parliament called Charles II (reigned 1660–85) back to the throne [7], it was taken for granted that he would rule in Scotland too. However, some of the extreme

CONNECTIONS

See also
The age of Marlborough

In other volumes
Scotland 1314-1560 (26)
The English Reformation (26)
Elizabeth and the Armada (26)
The Stuarts and Parliament 1603-42 (26)
The Commonwealth and Protectorate (26)

1 After the death of Henry II of France in 1559 (shown here), the French crown passed to Francis, the husband of Mary, Queen of Scots. This association of the Scottish queen with Catholic France weakened her popularity in Scotland; she adhered to her foreign tastes even after she returned to her home country in 1560. Her marriage to Darnley, also a Catholic, in 1565, was an attempt to overawe the Protestant opposition of Knox and Murray.

2 Mary's execution (shown here) took place in England in 1587, on the reluctant orders of her cousin Elizabeth. Mary had been driven out of Scotland in 1568 after the death of her cousin and husband Darnley, who had ordered the murder of Mary's Italian favourite, David Rizzio, in 1566. Elizabeth imprisoned Mary, who was also the heir to the English throne, for many years to prevent her from endangering Elizabeth's foreign and religious policies.

3 John Knox compiled, with other Calvinist ministers, *The First Booke of Discipline* (1560) which was the blueprint for the creed and constitution of the Protestant Church in Scotland. It decreed a hierarchy of Church courts, substantial stipends for ministers of the new Church, and proposed a generous programme of public education. This last had only limited success because the nobility refused to surrender enough of the old Church's wealth to finance it.

4 The revised prayer book was introduced by Charles I in 1637 and caused widespread disturbances. Much of this was against its imposition on Scottish congregations, but many Scots also regarded the book as a source of dangerous innovations. Popular unrest led to the Covenant of 1638 – a signed agreement to defend the reformed religion. The rebellion of the Covenanters culminated in the First Bishops' War in 1639 which was peacefully settled in the same year. However, the Scottish assembly, organized to resolve the conflict, and the Scottish Parliament openly defied the king. Charles was refused funds for his army by the Short Parliament, and his forces were defeated in the Second Bishops' War in 1640.

Presbyterian Whiggamore Party refused to accept any government not chosen by them; this and Charles's policy of re-establishing episcopacy led to disturbances. In this period the Scottish economy became dependent on trade with England. Scotland had to take part in English wars, even when the opponents were The Netherlands (1665–7, 1672–4), its main trading partner, and economic nationalism in France and Sweden further deprived Scotland of overseas markets.

The Revolution of 1688–9 against the Catholicizing policy of James II (VII) (reigned 1685–8) was, like the Restoration, made in England and accepted in Scotland. But there was a larger and more effective resistance group this time, particularly in the Highlands, where many preferred James to the new King William III (reigned 1689–1702) because of William's reliance in Scotland on the unpopular house of Argyll. These Highland Jacobites, or supporters of the Stuart (as the Stewarts became known after 1603) line, defeated William's army in 1689 at the Battle of Killiecrankie in the southern Highlands, but were prevented by a regiment of Covenanters defending Dunkeld from breaking through into the Lowlands. Later, the remaining Jacobite clans were brought to temporary submission by the Glencoe massacre in February 1692 [8].

Events leading to the Union

With the failure of William III and the next ruler, Anne (reigned 1702–14), to produce an heir, there was a possibility that the Scottish Parliament might bring back James rather than accept the Hanoverian successor chosen by England. This reasoning seems to have persuaded the English to accept the idea of uniting the parliaments of the two countries. The increasing dependence on trade with England meant that economic sanctions could be used to compel the Scots to accept a union. There was a period of increased interest in the Jacobite cause, and hostility to England in the early 1700s, but in 1707 economic generosity by England and political generosity by Scotland brought about the union of the parliaments in Westminster [9], although leaving the laws and church systems of the countries distinct.

The English and Scottish Crowns were united in 1603 when James VI was crowned James I of England. But James was not able to effect a parliamentary union of the two kingdoms.

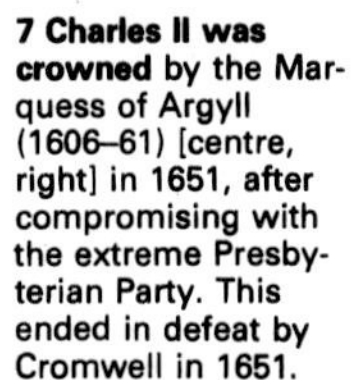

5 James Graham, Earl of Montrose (1612–50), was a leader of the Covenanters in the Bishops' Wars, although later, in the Civil War, he campaigned brilliantly for the king in Scotland.

6 General Monck (1608–70) commanded the English army in Scotland under the Protectorate. He took his army to London and made possible the restoration of the monarchy in 1660, with Charles II as king.

7 Charles II was crowned by the Marquess of Argyll (1606–61) [centre, right] in 1651, after compromising with the extreme Presbyterian Party. This ended in defeat by Cromwell in 1651.

8 The Massacre of Glencoe in 1692 took place after the Jacobite rising at Killiecrankie, three years earlier. William III demanded an oath of allegiance from the Highland clans, and the Macdonalds of Glencoe did not take it. As an example to other clans, 38 of the clan were slaughtered by government troops.

9 The Act of Union, in 1707, was made by commissioners from both countries and then passed into law by the separate parliaments. This process was relatively easy in England, but the Scottish Parliament needed a great deal of persuading by the Duke of Queensberry (1662–1711), shown attending Queen Anne's signing of the treaty.

The age of Marlborough

In January 1689 William III controlled the government and armed forces of England. He alone could maintain order and prevent confusion and was therefore in a strong enough position to prevent Parliament from imposing new restrictions on his power. The Declaration of Rights, read to William and Mary before they were offered the Crown, condemned James II's abuses of power and otherwise was so vague as to be unenforceable. William's position seemed as strong as that of Charles II in 1660, but with one crucial difference – Charles was granted a revenue for life; William was not, and as a result was to rely on Parliament for money.

England at war

From 1689 to 1697 and again from 1702 to 1713 England was involved in European wars of unprecedented scale. England declared war on France in 1689 because James II had fled there and hoped to recover his throne with the help of Louis XIV. But once involved, the English found themselves caught in the meshes of European power-politics. The English navy was already formidable but William III also turned the English army into the great fighting force that John Churchill, Duke of Marlborough (1650–1722) [3] was to use so brilliantly in a series of battles [4, 8]. Under Charles II England had been neither a major European power nor a military power, but by 1713 it was both. The War of the Spanish Succession concerned the future of the ailing Spanish Empire, and the treaty of Utrecht that ended the war in 1713 established Britain as the major colonial power.

The huge sums needed to sustain the war intensified the Crown's dependence on Parliament. Never before had the Commons voted so many taxes. The Triennial Act (1694) meant that new parliaments were called every three years, and were thus less easily managed by the government. Members of Parliament naturally wanted to know how their taxes had been spent, and demanded more and more detailed accounts. The Commons began to take a much more constructive attitude towards finance, voting taxes, not to spend on the war, but to pay interest on long-term loans from the public.

Parliamentary taxes constituted excellent security and, as a result, the government's credit was good. It could therefore borrow vast sums much more cheaply than could the other European monarchies. But the king's credit now depended so much on Parliament that its management became more important than ever. Those politicians who could control the Commons were in a position to make the king heed their advice.

The war also led to a great expansion of both the armed forces and the revenue administration. Ministers thus had many more rewards at their disposal than in the past; they used offices and pensions to buy support in and control of the Commons.

Whigs and Tories

Because the government had to borrow more money, those institutions that could lend on a large scale became increasingly powerful. These included the great trading companies and the Bank of England, established in 1694 [5]. The rise of this "moneyed interest" broke the landowners' traditional monopoly of political power. Country gentlemen saw

CONNECTIONS

See also
The Restoration of the Stuarts
Pepys's London

In other volumes
Science and technology 1500-1700 (29)
The age of Louis XIV (29)
Art and architecture in the 17th century (34)

1 William III (*r.* 1689–1702) **and Mary** (*r.* 1689–94) **were invited jointly to the throne in order to save the country from James II's Catholicism; William, who had been fighting Louis XIV for many years in The Netherlands, saw English naval strength as vital for him to defeat France permanently. This print shows him holding a globe on which Belgium, England and Scotland are marked as "free", and France and Spain are "to be freed".**

2 The Quakers, whose Synod is shown in session, were one of several Protestant sects that had sprung up in England by 1660 and asked only for toleration. Before 1640, although there had been disputes about the form of the Church of England, only the most extreme questioned the need for a single national Church. Anglican magistrates and clergy regarded the new sects as socially and politically subversive – Quakers refused to doff their hats to their social superiors – and so Dissenters were persecuted sporadically under Charles II. The persecution ended with the 1689 Toleration Act, although Dissenters were still excluded from public office.

3 John Churchill, Duke of Marlborough, owed his rise first to the favour of James II and then to the great influence of his own wife Sarah Jennings (1660–1744) over her close friend Anne, James's younger daughter; Anne became queen when William died (1702). It was Marlborough's great credit with Anne, more than his as yet unproven military genius, which led William to groom Marlborough from 1700 to 1702 to succeed him as leader of the great coalition against France.

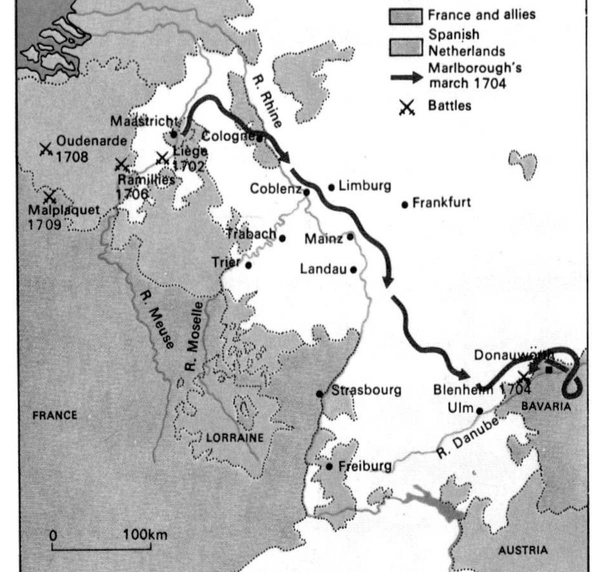

4 The War of the Spanish Succession (1702–13) saw England, Holland and Austria joined against France. At Blenheim (1704) after a quick march across Germany, Marlborough eliminated Bavaria, and prevented Louis from knocking out the Austrians by attacking Vienna. From 1705 Louis' efforts were concentrated in the southern Netherlands where, after some striking allied successes, at Ramillies (1706) and Oudenarde (1708) he was bogged down in a war of attrition until 1713.

the wars as a conspiracy to divert their hard-earned money into the pockets of bankers, contractors and civil servants. As the landowners were mostly Tories and the moneyed men mostly Whigs, this feeling added to the new bitterness of party politics. High taxation eventually made the wars unpopular and Marlborough himself was removed from his command and retired to Blenheim Palace [Key] as the result of a political vendetta, soon after a sweeping Tory election victory in 1710.

The other great political issue of the period 1689–1714 was religion. The Toleration Act of 1689 allowed most Protestant Dissenters [2] to worship freely but not to hold public office. The Church of England lost its monopoly of religious worship and of education. In 1695 the clergy also lost the last vestiges of their control over the press. Even so, the universities were still closed to Dissenters. The rigid Anglicans, concentrated in the Tory Party, bitterly resented this erosion of the Church's authority. They attacked Dissenting schools and occasional conformity (whereby a Dissenter took the sacrament in an Anglican church in order to qualify for office). The Tories' views might be reactionary but they had a great deal of popular support. In 1710 Dr Henry Sacheverell was impeached by the Commons after an intemperate sermon. The sermon sold a hundred thousand copies, Sacheverell became a popular hero and his Whig prosecutors were routed in the general election of 1710 [6].

The whirl of party politics

That particular period experienced the most vigorous electoral politics seen in England before 1832. The electorate was volatile and independent – and predominantly Tory. Other than the support of the moneyed interest the Whigs had one great electoral asset, fear of Jacobitism – of a return of Catholic rule if James II's son could seize power. The Whigs exploited this fear after the failure of the Jacobite rising of 1715. They had already won over the new king, the Hanoverian George I (1660–1727) [7]. But after the political excitement of Anne's reign came the relative political stagnation of the age of Walpole and the Whig supremacy.

KEY

Blenheim Palace, which stands in a beautiful park in Oxfordshire, was designed for Marlborough by John Vanbrugh (1664–1726). It testified to the gratitude of Parliament to a great general and to the profitability of high office.

5

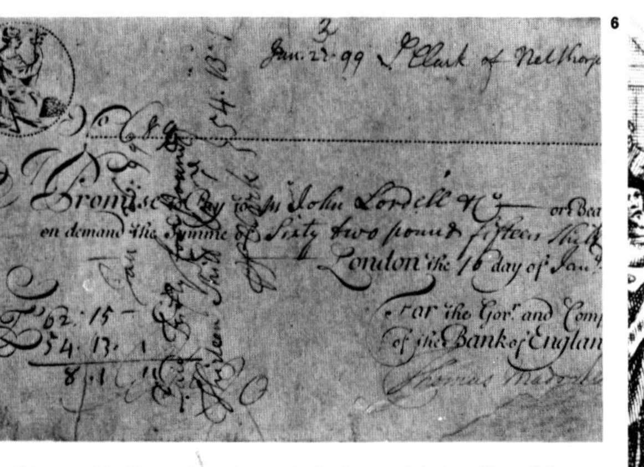

5 An early bank-note issued by the Bank of England in 1699 is illustrative of the bank's steadily growing capital. The Bank of England was one of the first commercial banking companies to be established in England. It was originally incorporated to lend the government £1,200,000, and empowered to issue paper money. It established the National Debt as a means of financing the war, leaving the debt for later generations to pay.

6

6 Henry Sacheverell (*c.* 1674–1724) became famous in 1709 for his sermon "The perils of false brethren", in which he stated that subjects should offer no resistance to their governments, and he criticized the Glorious Revolution of 1688–9 as an act of resistance to the divinely sanctioned monarch. In particular he violently opposed the toleration of Dissenters, arguing for a strong episcopacy, and by implication supported the agreement ("league") by which Louis promised to help James II to regain his throne. The Whigs impeached Sacheverell for sedition but the London mob rioted on his behalf and sympathy for him contributed to the Tory electoral victory in 1710.

7

7 The ceiling of the Painted Hall now in the Royal Naval College at Greenwich depicts the two foreign rulers who symbolized England's deliverance from Catholic rule: William III and George I (*r.* 1714–27). The latter was named heir to the throne after it became clear that Anne would leave no heir. The ceiling was painted by James Thornhill (1675–1734) and the dining hall is one of the most magnificent frescoed rooms in Britain.

8 The allied victory at Blenheim was made possible by two principal factors. The first of these was Marlborough's bold tactics. The French centre was weak and relied on marshy ground between the rival armies to impede the progress of the English and Austrian forces. But Marlborough's cavalry picked and floundered its way across with the aid of planks and brushwood and then routed the French infantry. The second factor was guile – even deceit – which Marlborough used to hoodwink the English and Dutch governments into allowing their troops to give battle so far from home.

8

England under the Hanoverians

England of the Hanoverian period, which began on 18 September 1714, with the arrival of Georg Ludwig (1660–1727), Elector of Hanover, at Greenwich to become George I of England [1], was a country generally free from the turbulence of the seventeenth century and the social and intellectual ferment of the nineteenth. Its apparent stability and prosperous complacency were revealed in politics, in religion, in commerce and in letters; the reigns of both George I and George II (reigned 1727–60) exhibited an external, though superficial, calmness that rested on the settlement of old quarrels at home and expanding power, naval and trading, overseas. Samuel Johnson (1709–84) [Key] represented the age, in his rational thought, political conservatism, and dry religious orthodoxy.

The Hanoverian succession

George I knew no English when he came to the throne. Both he and his son were more interested in Hanover than in England. George II was the last English monarch to lead his army into battle in Europe, at Dettingen in 1743. They both spent much of their time out of England, so that the House of Hanover did not become fully naturalized until the reign of George III (reigned 1760–1820).

Yet the royal court remained the centre of social life and of politics, the source of the patronage that was the cement of the political structure. The strife of the Civil Wars and the party rancour of the age of Queen Anne (reigned 1702–14) gave way to the politics of consensus, presided over by the Whig oligarchy established between 1721 and 1742 when Robert Walpole (1676–1745) [3] served as first minister.

The Whig politicians who had backed the Hanoverian succession undertook a long period of effectively one-party rule. The Jacobite uprisings of 1715 and 1745, attempting to restore the Stuarts to the throne, were dismal failures and tainted Toryism with disaffection and rebellion. The Whig landed gentry fused its interests with the court and the great merchant-financiers [2,6] and gained a stranglehold on the House of Commons and government service. Elections [5] remained unruly affairs, but the tiny electorate, the heavy cost of fighting elections (more or less direct bribery of the voters was common practice), and the large number of rotten and "pocket" boroughs kept the House of Commons under the control of the Whig government managers. The most famous and untiring of these was the Duke of Newcastle (1693–1768), who was Secretary of State (1724–48) and first minister (1754–62).

The growth of the empire and the expansion of trade and industry meant that the civil service became more elaborate. The Treasury, the Customs and Excise, the Admiralty and the War Office all expanded, and the dispensers of royal patronage often rewarded the place-hunting "friends" of the government with jobs in these departments.

The growth of the cabinet system

The cabinet began to develop as the main organ of government under the Hanoverians. Walpole, often considered to be the first prime minister (the term is still an unofficial one), bypassed the old Cabinet Councils

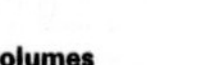

CONNECTIONS

See also
The agricultural revolution
Scotland in the 18th century
Pitt, Fox and the call for reform

In other volumes
Europe: economy and society, 1700-1800 (29)
The Enlightenment (29)
European literature in the 18th century (34)
Georgian art and architecture (34)

1 George I, aged 54 on his accession to the English throne, became king by virtue of the Act of Settlement of 1701, which had made his mother, Sophia, Electress of Hanover, heir to Anne's throne. This was done to prevent a return of the Stuart line. George, who had ruled as a despot in Hanover, had little liking for the English people or their liberal constitution and left the day-to-day running of affairs to his ministers.

2 Marine insurance companies, such as Sun-Fire, whose sign is shown here, were important to the development and the protection of 18th-century commerce. Most of these companies were financed as joint-stock enterprises. *Lloyd's List*, with news about merchant shipping, first published in 1734, is the oldest daily paper still published in London. Hanoverian prosperity rested on the profits of Britain's expanding trade empire.

3 Robert Walpole, here talking to Arthur Onslow (1691–1768), Speaker of the Commons, was defeated on his 1733 Excise Bill. He found that patronage alone could not guarantee a majority in the Commons as the substantial minority of "country gentlemen" was not bound to ministers by patronage. The development of the cabinet system was widely feared at this time and did not become fully established until the second half of the century. Walpole was criticized as a secretive, power-seeking man.

4 The War of Jenkins' Ear (1739–41) interrupted a long spell of peace for England. It was declared in response to the merchants' demand for protection at sea against the Spaniards. The ear, here being shown to Walpole by Capt. Jenkins, was allegedly torn off by Spanish coastguards. The war was fought mainly at sea near to the Spanish colonies, and although Britain won no important territorial advantages, the disruption hastened the decline of the Spanish Empire.

of privy councillors and relied on an inner cabinet of four or five of the Crown's principal ministers. They were not yet united by party – the resignation of the first minister rarely entailed that of any other – but the process had begun by which the cabinet and party were to oust the Crown and patronage from the centre of the political stage. The eighteenth century was the golden age of the mixed constitution, with a much-praised balance of King, Lords and Commons in the constitution or limited monarchy established by the "Whig revolution" of 1688–9.

The rise of Methodism

The Church of England was dormant following the bitter sectarian disputes of the previous two centuries. Protestant dissenters and Catholics were excluded from the universities as well as many public offices, unless they paid nominal allegiance to the established Church. Secure in its monopoly, the Church upheld a bland, unquestioning view of the truth of Christianity. Political obeisance to a powerful Whig patron was the way to a bishopric [8].

In such circumstances, it is not surprising that the most important religious movement of the century was the evangelical revival led by John Wesley (1703–91) [9]. His highly organized preaching tours, combined with the founding of "cells" in towns and villages, made Methodism by 1760 the most dynamic body of opinion in the country, and by 1800 there were more than 100,000 Methodists. The Anglican Church was implacably opposed to Wesley and no bishop would ordain his assistants for him. In 1784, he therefore broke with the Church and began to ordain his preachers himself.

Wesley appealed principally to the poor of a society marked by great inequalities. The Duke of Newcastle had an annual income of more than £50,000 from his estates in 12 counties, whereas a handloom weaver worked for less than a shilling (5p) a day. Nevertheless, although the mass of the people possessed neither the vote nor property, they had basic political rights – freedom from arbitrary arrest, trial by jury, the right to political demonstration – which were denied to most of their European contemporaries.

Samuel Johnson, essayist, poet, critic and lexicographer, gave the English language its first systematic and formal, if idiosyncratic, setting in his *Dictionary* of 1755. He was gregarious and nocturnal, and drank water and tea rather than wine. He lived comfortably but was never rich. In 1760 George III rewarded him with a civil-list pension of £300 a year. A resolute Tory, Johnson condemned the American rebels and defended the wealth and doctrines of the Church of England. He was renowned for his acerbic wit, recorded by James Boswell (1740–95), in the first great English biography.

5

5 Electoral violence, seen in this painting by William Hogarth (1697–1764), resulted from bribery of the voters, but it became less common as the century progressed. The Septennial Act (1716) greatly reduced the frequency of elections, and in 1761 only four elections were contested for county seats.

6

6 The Stock Exchange provided for the easy reinvestment of funds in new trading ventures or in industry. Since there was little social distinction drawn between wealth acquired in trade and that derived from land, the aristocracy happily contributed to the financial expansion that won for Britain the title "A nation of shopkeepers".

7 Cricket was widely played and was first organized on a county basis in the 18th century, thanks to the patronage of the great landowners. It epitomized the relative social harmony of rural areas, in contrast to the often violent towns, where riots such as the Gordon Riots of 1780 might occur. Lord's cricket ground was opened in 1787 by Thomas Lord for the White Conduit Club, later the Marylebone Cricket Club (MCC).

7

8

8 The bishops carried out few pastoral duties, dispensed much patronage and often lived richly while the over-worked lower clergy suffered. This cartoon suggests that the episcopal lifestyle had become quite unsuitable; 1,200 benefices in the 18th century had annual incomes of less than £20.

9

9 John Wesley offered the poor a promise of individual salvation, an idea that seemed to be genuinely egalitarian. His appeal to the personal worth of each individual quickened a response, especially in the new industrial towns of Wales and the north, where the Church of England was inactive.

The agricultural revolution

Historians have often described the changes that occurred in British farming during the course of the eighteenth and nineteenth centuries as an "agricultural revolution". The phrase was coined in the nineteenth century by those who saw comparable changes in the mode of production and social relationships on the land to what was happening in industry. More recent research has tended to emphasize the long drawn-out evolution of agricultural change and the varied pattern that it presents over the country as a whole. The earliest books on farming techniques had appeared in the early sixteenth century and enclosure had started in the thirteenth century, accelerating in the sixteenth century.

The results of new techniques

Whether or not the phrase "agricultural revolution" is an exaggeration, changes in British agriculture between, say, 1700 and 1870, were real and substantial. Greatly improved output, new crops, and improved techniques were matched by a number of important social developments.

Many of the changes in agricultural practice made wider use of established ideas. The use of rotation of crops, for example, particularly the utilization of root crops such as the turnip as a part of the rotation and a source of winter feed for animals, was known in the seventeenth century. Selective breeding of livestock was familiar to earlier generations but was impracticable under the open field system of agriculture where animals were herded together in the common field.

Agricultural historians have identified the hundred years before 1750 as one of slack demand for farm products because of an upward trend in harvests and a largely static population. From 1750 onward, however, a discernible rise in population and generally poorer harvests provided a stimulus to investment in agriculture and the application of fresh techniques in order to increase production. A number of pioneers, such as Jethro Tull (1674–1741), Charles "Turnip" Townshend (1674–1738), and Robert Bakewell (1725–95) popularized the new techniques. Probably the most important of these were the use of crop rotation, scientific breeding of animals, and the use of crops such as turnips and lucerne as animal fodder. These improved yields led to heavier and healthier animals – within the century the average weight of sheep sold in London nearly trebled and permitted the wintering of livestock on stored feed. New implements such as improved ploughs [7] and harrows, as well as Tull's revolutionary seed drill, contributed to the improvement of yields [2].

The effects of enclosure

Many of these techniques could not have been applied without reorganization of landholding. Enclosure of land [Key, 4] into self-contained units had been going on for centuries; more than one-third of England was enclosed by 1600, usually by agreement among local landowners. From the mid-eighteenth century, much land was enclosed through private Acts of Parliament. Enclosure involved creating separate holdings out of the medieval common and "open" fields. Generally it eliminated the inefficiency of farming strips in each field and the wasteful system of leaving one field fallow each year, and it also permitted farmers to experiment

CONNECTIONS

See also
England under the Hanoverians
The early Industrial Revolution

In other volumes
History of agriculture (7)
Farm stock breeding and management (8)
New farm technology (8)
Europe: economy and society, 1700-1800 (29)

1 Agricultural manuals and tracts helped to spread the use of new techniques among farmers from as early as the 16th century. During the late 18th century agricultural improvement became a fashionable concern: King George III (*r.* 1760–1820) himself ran a model farm at Windsor.

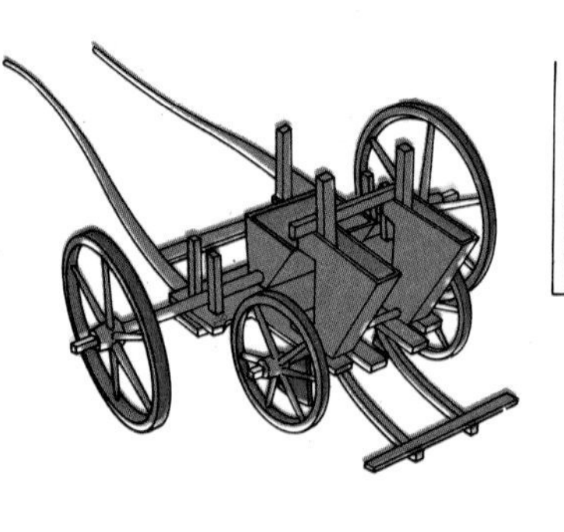

2 Jethro Tull's famous horse-drawn seed drill, first used in 1701, is regarded as having initiated the mechanization of agriculture. Before this invention, seed was laboriously broadcast by hand, which was a wasteful and uncertain procedure.

A
DISCOURS
OF
HUSBANDRIE
USED IN
Brabant and Flanders:
SHEWING
The wonderful improvement of Land there; and serving as a pattern for our practice in this
COMMON-WEALTH.

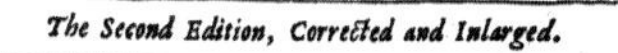

The Second Edition, Corrected and Inlarged.

LONDON,
Printed by *William Du-Gard*, dwelling in *Suffolk-lane*, near London-stone, *Anno Dom.* 1652.

3 Richard Weston's (1591–1652) *A Discours of the Husbandrie used in Brabant and Flanders* (1645) spread Flemish agricultural ideas among English farmers. It described methods of crop rotation and several techniques by which poor soils were improved.

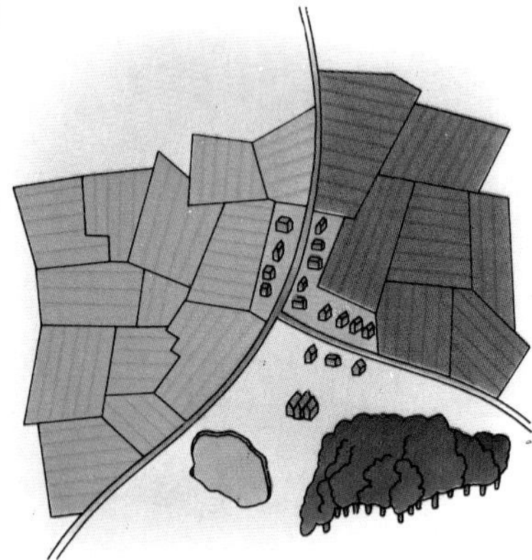

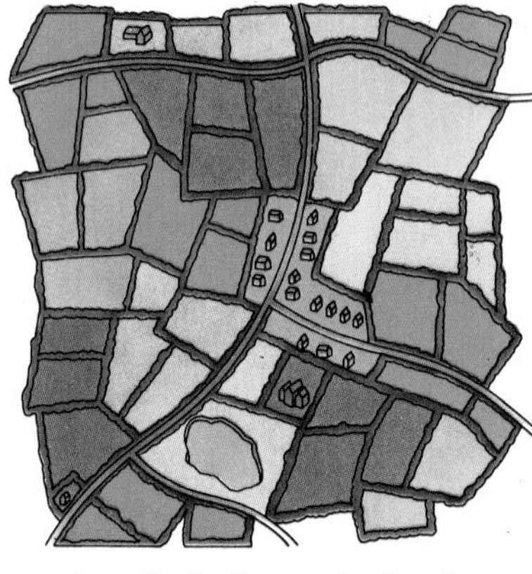

4 The effects of enclosure upon landholding can be seen from the plans of a typical parish. Before enclosure, many villages preserved the medieval layout of large open fields in which each inhabitant held by custom a few strips. The intention was to give everybody a share of good and bad land. But this meant that the land between each strip was wasted and involved unnecessary journeys between different fields. It was impossible to experiment with new techniques, and most people used a simple system of rotation that left one field fallow for a year. Enclosure consolidated holdings and permitted improved agriculture. The progressive farmers supported it, and those with large holdings often provided incentives in order to obtain better tenants at greater rents. After enclosure, all the land was divided up, and hedges were usually planted to mark the new field boundaries, in this way creating what is now the familiar English landscape.

5 The Game Laws restricted the taking of game to men of property. In 1671 freeholders with less than £100 worth of property and leaseholders with less than £150 were prohibited from taking deer, hares, rabbits, pheasants or partridges. As enclosure progressed, the areas in which labourers and smallholders could legitimately take game were still further reduced. Harsher game laws were introduced, including imprisonment, transportation and even death in the case of resistance to gamekeepers. Mantraps (such as the one shown) and spring-guns were used to deter poachers, and gamekeepers were given wide powers. But the 19th century saw a relaxation of these laws.

with new techniques on a consolidated holding. Nearly 3,000 enclosure acts were passed between 1751 and 1810, the largest number being passed during the Napoleonic Wars (1803–15) when, due to trade dislocation, food prices were at their highest [10].

Poverty and prosperity

The enclosures of this period were once believed to have contributed to the pauperization of the agricultural labourer by depriving him of his rights of grazing on the common and rendering his smallholding uneconomic. This view has now changed. Many smallholders remained and the number of families working on the land actually rose between 1750 and 1831. Migration did take place from the land, and many smallholders were pushed into the ranks of wage-labourers, but this was more the effect of population growth than of enclosure. Pauperization of the agricultural labourer arose from chronic rural unemployment and concomitantly depressed wage levels.

On the other hand, owners of large farms tended to prosper. The landed classes of the eighteenth century had ample wealth for housebuilding, the creation of rich collections, and foreign travel. The wealthier of their tenants and professional farmers were also able to build substantial farmhouses. That tireless observer of rural life, William Cobbett (1762–1835), among others, noticed that the social status of farmers had greatly improved by the 1820s, but that it had the effect of making them more distant from their employees. Much contemporary comment satirized the social pretensions of farmers and their families in the early nineteenth century. But it took several decades for the typical pattern of Victorian rural society – which was that of large landowners, tenant farmers, and landless labourers – to emerge.

Expansion of the cultivatable acreage and improved yields provided the food for a growing urban population. Precise production figures are not available, but Britain's ability to feed itself despite the virtual trebling of its population between 1750 and 1850 was not the least remarkable feature of the development of its economy.

Enclosure was generally completed with little serious disagreement. To obtain an Act of Parliament took time and required the agreement of many of the local landowners. The land also had to be accurately surveyed and the appropriate legal titles established. The allocation of land was usually fair. Each enclosure act appointed commissioners to distribute the land.

6

6 The "Pangborn Hog" was a gigantic prize pig reared on Tidmarsh Farm in Berkshire as a result of systematically controlled and scientific breeding. There were also new strains of other animals by selective breeding. Among the farmers who popularized new breeds of sheep was Robert Bakewell of Dishley, Leicestershire. He was so successful that he managed to double the amount of meat obtainable from each of his sheep.

7

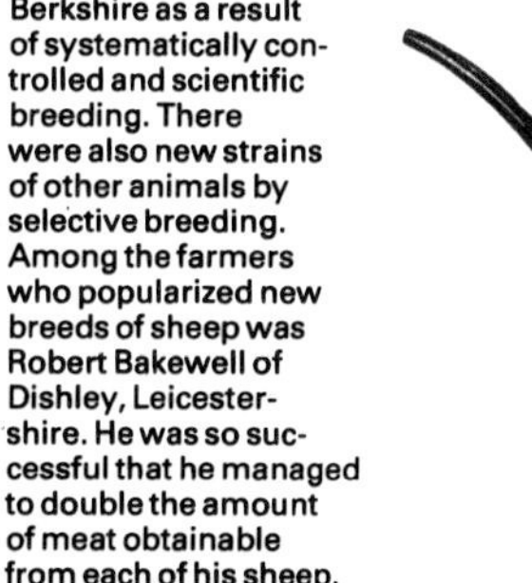

7 Agricultural improvements owed little to new machinery, apart from Tull's seed drill. But many small improvements were carried out on existing implements. An improved plough with a metal blade, for example, was produced in 1703, and wooden ploughs were gradually superseded. The Rotherham plough, shown here, included a metal blade and appeared in 1730.

8 Arthur Young (1741–1820) was a famous propagandist for the techniques of agricultural improvement in Britain. In his books and articles he argued that large-scale farming, using enclosure, the latest techniques and plentiful capital would greatly increase production. His writings provide historians with a rich source of information about the social, political and economic life of the 18th century.

8

9

9 Holkham Gatherings was the name given to a series of agricultural shows organized by Thomas Coke (1752–1842) of Holkham in Norfolk. Coke was a pioneer of agricultural improvement and, like many others, he was a propagandist for the new methods. He experimented with root crops, especially the swede, helped to improve breeds of cattle, sheep and pigs, and was the first to grow wheat instead of rye in western Norfolk.

10 Agricultural output increased during the 18th century as new methods of farming were introduced. Rapid population growth stimulated demand at home; exports also increased. Here the average annual export of corn is shown for each ten-year period. Domestic prices reached a peak at the time of the Napoleonic Wars but fell slightly after 1815. The protective Corn Laws kept prices up, but even when these were repealed, in 1846, farming remained prosperous.

10

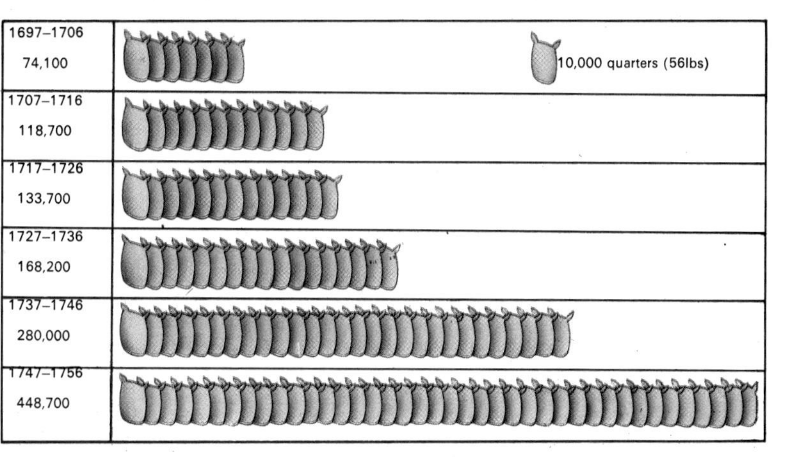

The English in Ireland

At the end of the Middle Ages, Ireland remained a partially conquered country in which opposed cultures coexisted uneasily. English influence was confined to the colonized counties around Dublin. Beyond that "Pale" were some 90 independent lordships, two-thirds of them ruled by Gaelic dynasts, the rest by gaelicized Anglo-Norman lords. The only significant governmental function was defence, and this was entrusted to the FitzGeralds of Kildare.

The Reformation and anglicization

The weakness of the state was of merely local importance until the Reformation, by altering England's relations with Europe, gave Ireland a new strategic significance. After 1534, an attempt was made to improve international security by extending English control in Ireland. Direct rule was introduced on the basis of imported governors, civil servants [1] and armies, but experience soon revealed that control could not rest on military conquest alone and there followed an associated programme of anglicization.

Both Gaelic and Anglo-Norman lords resisted encroachments on their autonomy, and the situation was complicated by the tenacity with which both natives and settlers adhered to their Catholicism.

The conquest was poorly financed, piecemeal and protracted. It was brought to completion only when the outbreak of war between England and Catholic Spain made Ireland a strategic liability. In the Nine Years War (1595–1603), an Ulster-based confederacy of Gaelic lords led by Hugh O'Neill (*c.* 1540–1616) was defeated, and the incoming James I (reigned 1603–25) became the first English king to rule all Ireland. Thereafter, anglicization proceeded quickly.

The self-exile of the defeated northern leaders made possible the systematic "plantation" of Ulster with English and Scots settlers [4, 7]. The discriminatory enforcement of English property law allowed a widespread public and private expropriation of the Irish to take place elsewhere. A sizeable group of immigrant Protestant landowners gradually developed. Their influence was contested by the older Catholic colonists, who vowed loyalty to the Crown and sought guarantees of their property rights but were rebuffed in the 1630s when Lord Deputy Wentworth (1593–1641), later the Earl of Strafford [5], confiscated a proportion of their land to further a colonizing scheme he was promoting in Connaught.

Protestant conquest

When the Ulster Irish rose in rebellion in 1641, the Catholic colonists joined them. Both were united in fearing that the growing influence of the English Parliament and the Scots would overturn the practical toleration of Catholicism in Ireland. There was little unity of purpose, because the colonists, who possessed one-third of Ireland, had much to lose, while the Irish, joined by returning exiles from Europe, had much to gain. The English Civil Wars created disabling divisions on the English side, but after Charles I (reigned 1625–49) had been executed, Oliver Cromwell (1599–1658) conquered Ireland easily and ruthlessly [6]. A vast expropriation followed, in which no distinction was made between the Gaelic Irish and the

CONNECTIONS

See also
Ireland from Union to Partition

In other volumes
Medieval Ireland (26)
Irish culture to 1850 (34)
Irish culture since 1850 (35)

1 Edmund Spenser (1552-99) served as a minor official in Ireland and acquired plantation lands in County Cork where he wrote much of *The Faerie Queene*. His grandson was designated an "Irish papist" by the Cromwellians, deprived of his estate and transplanted to Connaught with many other Catholics.

2 Thomas Lee (*d.* 1601), here fancifully portrayed as an Irish knight dressed for bogland terrain, was one of the many English adventurers who sought their fortunes in 16th-century Ireland. Others included Richard Grenville (*c.* 1542-91), Humphrey Gilbert (*c.* 1539-83) and Walter Raleigh (*c.* 1552-1618).

3 Crannogs, artificial islands of brushwood, peat, logs and stones sometimes surrounded by a timber palisade, mostly date from the early Bronze Age, although Neolithic remains have been found in some. They provided a secure home for the more important families in low-lying and marshy areas. Some were still inhabited in Ulster during the 16th century.

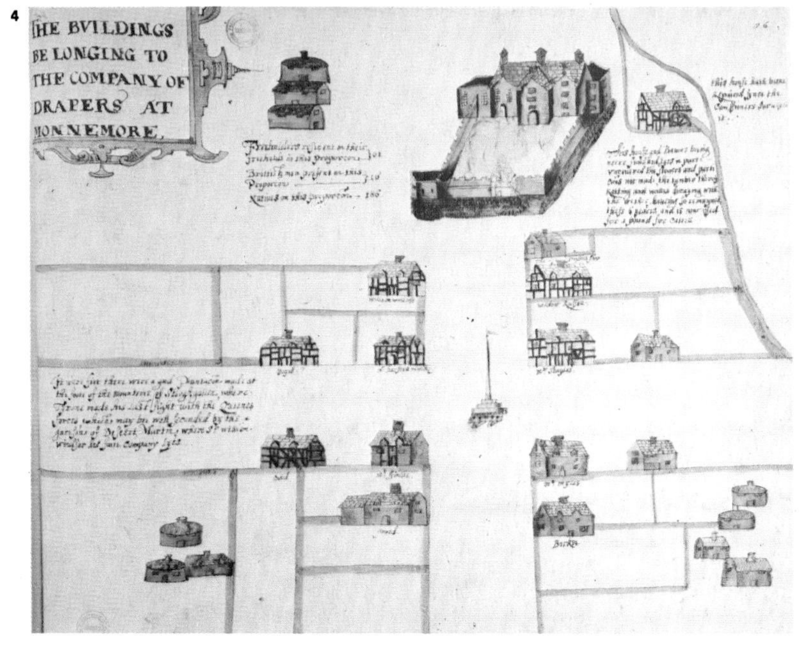

4 The village, in plantation areas, was not only a unit of defence, but a symbol of civilization. In Ulster, as this contemporary map detail shows, they were composed of neat timber-framed houses and cottages that contrasted sharply with the native Irish settlements in which wattle and turf houses clustered together.

5 The independence of the Lord Lieutenant of Ireland, the Earl of Strafford, posed a threat to the power of the English and Scottish parliaments when they joined forces against the Crown in 1640. He was charged with treason, the Irish Parliament readily attested to his misgovernment and the discontents of three kingdoms converged to lead to his execution.

Catholic colonial community. This was not accompanied by systematic settlement however, and existing Protestant settlers benefitted largely.

When Charles II (reigned 1660–85) was restored in 1660, his dependence upon Protestant support ensured that only token modifications of this arrangement were possible. But the fact that his brother and heir, James II (reigned 1685–8), was a Catholic gave hope of redress, and Catholics in Ireland rallied to James's support when he was deposed in 1688, while Protestants transferred their allegiance to William of Orange (reigned 1689–1702) [Key].

The Protestants were confirmed in their ownership of Irish land, and the government confirmed in its power to rule Ireland without reference to the interests of its Catholic population. Protestant supremacy was secured by a system of laws designed to depress Catholics, and particularly the remaining Catholic landholders, rather than to suppress Catholicism. Important changes within the Catholic community followed. As the population increased steadily, and landlords responded to demand by letting their land in ever smaller units, settlers and natives gradually merged into a depressed peasantry. In the towns, by contrast, where economic activity was less affected by penal constraints, a Catholic middle class desirous of its full rights slowly developed.

Union with England

The privileged society of Irish Protestants quickly acquired local interest and ambitions. No longer needing English support to uphold their position, they came to resent English control. Their claims for recognition of Ireland's legislative independence were conceded in 1782.

Circumstances soon challenged the basis of Protestant ascendancy. Indeed, the growth of republican separatism produced an abortive rising in 1798 so that when the government proposed the political union of England and Ireland as the most secure arrangement, Irish Protestants recognized the scheme as the best means of protecting their position in the future [10]. In 1800, the Irish Parliament voted itself out of existence.

KEY

The Battle of the Boyne between James II and William of Orange in 1690 was fought for control of the English throne. The battle was part of a wider European conflict and the armies were international, but it incidentally decided the future of Ireland. William's victory established a Protestant domination that excluded the Catholic descendants of English settlers from the colonial community and led them to assimilate with the Irish.

6

6 When Cromwell landed in Ireland in 1649 his purpose was not only conquest but also revenge for the reputed massacre of Protestants in 1641. This vengeance was exacted on the town of Drogheda (shown here) although its commander was English, its garrison was Royalist and the townspeople had played no part in the rebellion of 1641. The inhumanity of Cromwell's campaign remains impressed upon Irish folk memory.

7

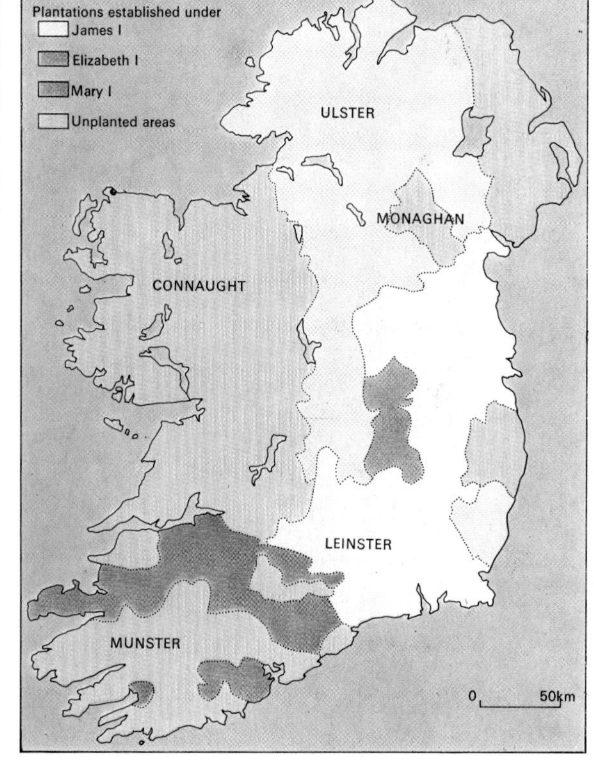

7 The character of settlement varied widely. In all planted areas, settlers were interspersed among natives, but in Ulster, particularly in the unofficial, Scottish-based northeastern settlements, they were a fair reflection of society; elsewhere the lower classes were greatly under-represented. In unplanted areas, land ownership changed radically: in 1641 Catholics held 59 per cent of Irish land; by 1703 their share had fallen to 14 per cent.

8

8 The impressive classical façade of the Custom House in Dublin symbolizes the prosperity of the privileged in the late 18th century and suggests the extravagance of their life-style.

9

9 Edmund Burke (1729–97), the statesman and philosopher, left Ireland as a young man, although his parliamentary championship of the interests of the American colonists was informed by an Irishman's understanding of their situation.

10

10 By the Act of Union, the centuries-old Irish Parliament exchanged its recently won legislative independence for Irish representation at Westminster. Its passage was widely believed to have been procured by bribery. In fact Irish Protestants chose to surrender their power to a protective England of their own accord. Despite Protestant identification with England, the English persistently regarded them as Irish, as this contemporary cartoon suggests.

Scotland in the 18th century

With the passing of the Act of Union in 1707, Scotland ceased to be an independent country and became part of Great Britain. Sixteen Scottish peers were elected to join the House of Lords (English membership 190) and 45 MPs sat in the House of Commons (English membership 513) at Westminster. Scottish MPs were notoriously pliable to the government's will at Westminster. The effective management of Scottish affairs in Parliament passed to government "managers" – the Dukes of Argyll for much of the century and thereafter usually the lord advocates, of whom Henry Dundas (1742–1811) William Pitt the Younger's confidant, was the most famous and effective.

The Jacobite rebellions

Enemies of the Union were few and far between, except for the Jacobites who supported the exiled House of Stewart's claim to the throne. In 1715, the Earl of Mar (1675–1732), a former supporter of the Union whose political ambitions had been blocked, attempted to raise the country for James Edward, the Old Pretender (1688–1766), James II's son. The rising won most support in the Highlands, but petered out after the inconclusive Battle of Sheriffmuir in November 1715 [1].

In 1714, the Young Pretender, Prince Charles Edward Stewart (1720–88), made a second attempt on the throne. In August he landed in Inverness-shire from a French ship and proclaimed his father King of Scotland and England. Even among the Highland clans only a minority followed him, and despite initial successes in which he took Edinburgh and defeated a Hanoverian army at Prestonpans, Charles was relying upon English Jacobite and French support when he marched on London in November [3]. The Jacobite army reached Derby and after some hesitation, in the face of mounting opposition forces under the Duke of Cumberland (1721–65), turned back northwards.

In April 1746, Cumberland caught up with Charles at Culloden [4] where the Jacobite army, outnumbered and poorly organized, was heavily defeated. The rebellion was finally crushed and Charles forced to flee back to France. The Union remained intact. Even the Jacobites had primarily wanted to regain the British throne for the Stewarts rather than to re-establish Scottish independence. With their defeat there was no further challenge to Westminster government for nearly half a century, and in the aftermath of Culloden the power of the Highlanders was broken for ever.

Economic consequences of the Union

The satisfaction that most Scots felt for the Union in the eighteenth century rested largely on an economic base and the new markets opened up by the Union with England. Although there was little dramatic change in the condition of the country until after 1760, even in the first half of the century food became more plentiful, the cattle trade with England expanded and linen emerged as the first major Scottish industry.

The tobacco trade, too, became an important source of prosperity to Glasgow and the west of Scotland when in the 1740s Scottish merchants secured bulk contracts to supply tobacco to France. The link forged with Virginia remained important until after

CONNECTIONS

See also
Scotland from 1560 to the Act of Union
England under the Hanoverians
The British Labour Movement to 1868
Scotland in the 19th century

In other volumes
Scotland to the Battle of Bannockburn (26)
Scotland 1314-1560 (16)
Scottish culture to 1850 (34)
Scottish culture since 1850 (35)

1

1 After the Battle of Sheriffmuir the cause of the Old Pretender was doomed. The rebel prisoners were taken south to be tried by courts in Carlisle and London because it was feared that they would not be punished severely enough under Scottish law. Here one of the two executions of the rebels, that of Lord Derwentwater (1689–1716), is shown.

2 Rioting broke out in Glasgow in 1725 following the decision by Westminster to extend the tax on malt to include Scotland as well as England. An angry mob attacked the house of Campbell of Shawfield who had supported the measure in Parliament. It was essentially an anti-government riot and not pro-Jacobite.

2

3

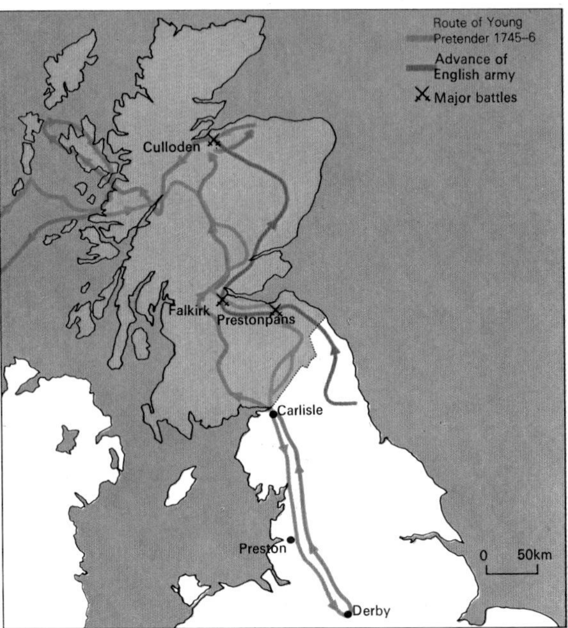

4

3 Prince Charles's march through Scotland and into England was almost unopposed. His army took Edinburgh without a shot, routed a Hanoverian army at Prestonpans, captured Carlisle and marched on London. But after reaching Derby, the Prince retreated northwards on 6 December 1745.

4 The bloody battle at Culloden, near Inverness, on 16 April 1746 was an overwhelming victory for the Hanoverian forces and effectively broke the Jacobite cause forever. In its aftermath many of the defeated clansmen were butchered by the victorious army under the Duke of Cumberland.

the American Revolution (1775–83).

Towards the end of the century economic change became more rapid and far-reaching. In the Lowlands landowners and their tenants began enclosures, turnip husbandry and more intensive forms of farming both for animals and grain. By 1790 this had transformed the Lothians and was beginning to have an impact elsewhere. In the Highlands the "crofting system" was introduced whereby tenants had smallholdings along the shore and spent part of their time fishing or gathering seaweed ('kelp') from which an industrial alkali was manufactured. Everywhere in the countryside population increased rapidly, many migrated to gain employment in the towns or settled round the new industries such as Carron Iron Works (founded 1759) or the cotton mills at New Lanark (founded 1785) [9].

The Scottish Enlightenment

During this period of economic prosperity, Edinburgh flourished exceedingly. Its enterprising town council planned a New Town focused on Princes Street and George Street; by 1800 this was attracting fashionable and middle-class families to its splendid homes in large numbers [Key]. The Scottish universities, especially Edinburgh and Glasgow, gained a worldwide reputation. Thinkers such as the philosopher David Hume (1711–76), economist Adam Smith (1723–90), the poet Robert Burns (1759–96), painters and architects such as Henry Raeburn (1756–1823) and Robert Adam (1728–92) and inventors such as James Watt (1736–1819), created "Scottish Enlightenment" of learning and ingenuity without parallel in the past [6, 8].

Not everyone, however, was convinced that the system was incapable of improvement. In the last decade of the century Scottish radical sympathizers with the French Revolution, especially the Friends of the People and the United Scotsmen began to make demands for a more democratic form of government [7]. Dundas and Pitt suppressed them as they had also suppressed English radical clubs, but in the nineteenth century the radicals' challenge proved more enduring than that of the Jacobites.

KEY

Charlotte Square in Edinburgh was the most splendid of the squares built in the New Town in the 18th century. The planning and construction of the New Town reflects the growing wealth and prosperity of the professional classes in 18th-century Edinburgh. Robert Adam was the main architect of this square and the elegant, classical style for which he is famous dominates the New Town.

5

5 The Royal Bank of Scotland was founded in 1727 largely because the Bank of Scotland's directors were suspected of Jacobitism. Even today the rival banks issue different notes.

6

Encyclopædia Britannica;

OR, A

DICTIONARY

OF

ARTS and SCIENCES,

COMPILED UPON A NEW PLAN.

IN WHICH

The different SCIENCES and ARTS are digefted into diftinct Treatifes or Syftems;

AND

The various TECHNICAL TERMS, &c. are explained as they occur in the order of the Alphabet.

ILLUSTRATED WITH ONE HUNDRED AND SIXTY COPPERPLATES.

By a SOCIETY of GENTLEMEN in SCOTLAND.

IN THREE VOLUMES.

VOL. I.

EDINBURGH:

Printed for A. BELL and C. MACFARQUHAR;

And fold by COLIN MACFARQUHAR, at his Printing-office, Nicolfon-ftreet.

M.DCC.LXXI.

6 The *Encyclopaedia Britannica*, compiled by a "society of gentlemen", first began to come off the Edinburgh presses in weekly numbers in December 1768. The editor was William Smellie (1740–95), a local printer, and the work aimed to provide "a dictionary of the arts and sciences". The three volumes of the first edition were completed in 1771 and an expanded second edition was begun in 1776.

7

7 Thomas Muir (1765–98), an Edinburgh lawyer and leader of the Friends of the People, was tried for sedition before Lord Braxfield in 1793. This was one of a series of trials held in the wake of the French Revolution that were aimed at Jacobin radical societies. After a hearing notorious for the violent bias of Braxfield, Muir was sentenced to transportation to Botany Bay for 14 years.

8

8 The school system in Scotland was the cornerstone of the great flowering of intellectual life in the late 18th century that was the Scottish Enlightenment. The ability to read and write was much more widespread than in England, and in many areas the rural parish school (supported by a tax levied on local landowners) educated both rich and poor. In the Highlands and towns, however, the parish system was inadequate and would often be supplemented by the wealthy with private tuition. The universities in the 18th century, in particular Edinburgh, flourished and established an eminent tradition in law, medicine and philosophy.

9

9 The new technology of Richard Arkwright (1732–92), made it possible to spin cotton fibres by water power. Arkwright introduced his new technique into Scotland at New Lanark (shown here) because he wished to undercut English labour costs. In 1799 the mills were sold to Robert Owen (1771–1858). Owen made the community at New Lanark world-famous for his pioneering social reforms: in working conditions, housing and education.

The early Industrial Revolution

Britain was the first industrial nation in the world. From the middle of the eighteenth century, a number of factors launched Britain into a period of self-sustaining economic growth by the first decade of the nineteenth century. However, the origins of the Industrial Revolution in Britain lay in the pre-industrial period; by the middle of the eighteenth century there was already a thriving commercial economy, with a growing population, developing agriculture, and expanding trade both at home and abroad.

Population growth

The growth of Britain's population from the mid-eighteenth century was not directly caused by industrialization although a large workforce was an essential factor in the development of industry. A run of good harvests in the first half of the century, low food prices, favourable climatic conditions, the decline of plague and a number of minor improvements in health all contributed to lower death rates and a consequent rise in population [2]. By the end of the eighteenth century, birth-rates began to rise, too, as people in the industrial towns were able to marry earlier and to have, and keep, more children. Unlike Ireland, where population growth led to impoverishment and, ultimately, to famine, Britain's commercial and agricultural prosperity meant that a growing population contributed to increasing demand for products of every kind. Increased consumption was a stimulus to industrial innovation and methods of production.

In the past, periods of agricultural expansion had been checked by harvest failure, population level and economic downturn. By the middle of the eighteenth century, the profits of thriving overseas trade enabled landowners to borrow capital to increase agricultural production [5]. With increasing demand and prices for foodstuffs, agricultural expansion followed. The enclosure movement grouped the old open fields and common lands into individual, more efficient units, on which more productive techniques could be applied, such as improved animal husbandry, new root crops and the first agricultural machines. Enclosure, secured through Parliamentary Acts, had affected about 20 per cent of the area of England by 1845. Capital was required to make the most of enclosure and it led to many smaller farms being amalgamated into larger holdings. Contrary to common myth, enclosure did not depopulate the countryside, but often increased the demand for agricultural labour.

Increased demand

The continued profitability of foreign trade [1], particularly as the colonies grew, provided the capital for increases in production to meet demand at home and abroad. One of the first industries to feel this increased demand was mining, with the need for more domestic and industrial fuel. Output was increased 400 per cent in the course of the eighteenth century through the use of steam pumping engines to keep mines from flooding. Coal was an important raw material for many industrial processes as well as the fuel for steam power. Coal and iron together laid the foundations for the development of industry [4]. The iron industry of the early eighteenth century depended on charcoal for smelting and had a relatively small output.

CONNECTIONS

See also
England under the Hanoverians
The agricultural revolution
The British Labour Movement to 1868

In other volumes
Technology of the Industrial Revolution (9)
Europe: economy and society, 1700-1800 (29)
Exploration and science 1750-1850 (29)
The Industrial Revolution (29)
International economy 1700-1800 (30)
Industrialization 1870-1914 (31)

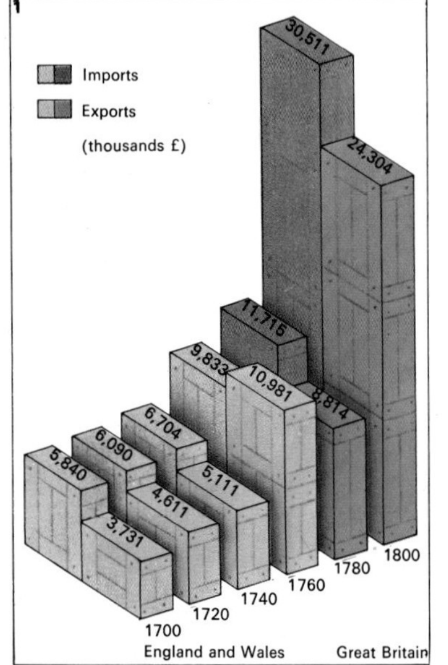

1 Industry was stimulated by growing demand, both at home and abroad. Britain's overseas trade experienced a rapid expansion from the 1680s, providing new market opportunities and the capital for investment in new techniques. New colonial markets acquired after the Seven Years War proved lucrative, as Britain engaged in the "Triangular Trade" carrying factory goods to Africa and the West Indies, transporting slaves across the Atlantic and bringing back colonial produce to Europe. Britain's largest export commodity in the first half of the 18th century was woollen textiles, but this was later overtaken by cotton.

2 Europe's population increased from the 1750s, and despite some appalling conditions in towns (here shown at one extreme in one of William Hogarth's Gin Lane pictures), mortality rates declined. The cause of this is not fully understood but may have been related to the end of plague epidemics after 1700 and improvements in hygiene after 1800, such as the availability of cheap soap, easily washable cotton clothing and improved water supply. Increased population because of earlier marriage and larger families provided a growing market for cheap industrial products and also the necessary ready supply of labour.

3 Mills driven by water provided the motive force for many processes before the Industrial Revolution, including grinding corn and spinning yarn. A flourishing woollen industry already existed in areas where water power was readily available, such as the Cotswolds, East Anglia and the West Riding of Yorkshire. Many early machines could be driven by water power and the first phase of industrialization was based almost entirely upon the use of water-driven machinery. Both the cotton and woollen industries developed on the slopes of the Pennines with abundant water power. It was only with the development of efficient steam power after 1776 that industry began to concentrate upon the coalfields and no longer had to depend on the hilly regions. The use of coal and invention of coke-smelting enabled industry to expand and escape the problems of a critical shortage of wood for fuel. However, the change to steam was gradual.

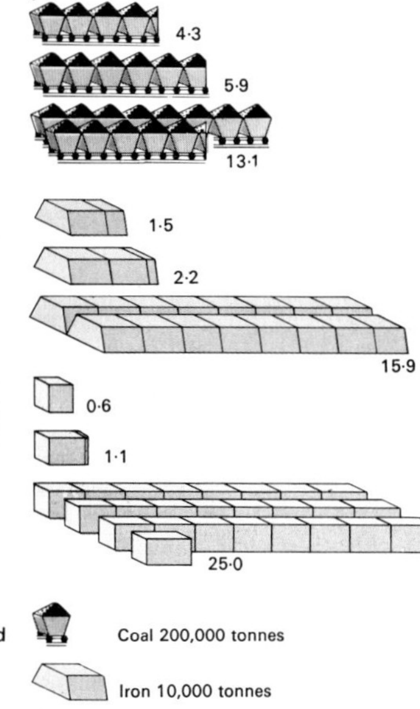

4 The most striking developments in 18th-century industry were shown in coal, textiles and iron production. Coal mining expanded with the rise of steam power, a growing population and improvements in communications. Wool output increased to meet domestic and foreign demand, but mainly using traditional processes. Cotton production grew dramatically with the use of machinery and steam power until it became Britain's principal export commodity. Iron production also increased rapidly with the introduction of coke-smelting. These developments were evidence of a broad expansion of techniques to meet opportunities presented by rapidly growing markets.

The discovery by Abraham Darby of coke-smelting at his Coalbrookdale works in the 1730s revolutionized the production of cheap iron and enabled it to be used in the first machines and iron structures.

Allied to these developments, there was a major advance in technological power following the patenting of the improved Boulton and Watt steam engines after 1774. They used much less fuel than earlier models. Beside pumping, Watt's steam engine of 1769 was harnessed to drive machinery.

Labour-saving machinery

After steam power, the most important innovations were associated with the growth of labour-saving machinery. They occurred most dramatically in the cotton industry, which witnessed technical breakthroughs in weaving (Kay's flying shuttle, 1733) then in spinning [Key] and gradually in other processes. The harnessing of steam power to machinery in the cotton industry led to the first factories in which the production processes were concentrated under one roof [7]. Although many factories still relied on water power [3], the development of the factory system in cotton foreshadowed the growth of the factory and the use of steam in other industries. Woollen production, for example, expanded mainly by using traditional methods such as water power. Gradually, however, the introduction of machinery and the use of steam power drew it towards the coalfields of the West Riding of Yorkshire.

Concentration of production needed both capital and cheap transport. Capital was provided out of the profits of agricultural improvement and overseas trade. Country banks, although subject to panics and bankruptcies, did provide a basic network of credit for industrial and agricultural development. By 1800 there were about 70 London banks and about 400 country banks, usually issuing their own notes. The Stock Exchange was founded in 1773.

Land transport remained slow and expensive for bulky products, in spite of the development of turnpikes. River transport was cheaper, but it was only with the development of the canal network that bulky products could be moved cheaply [6].

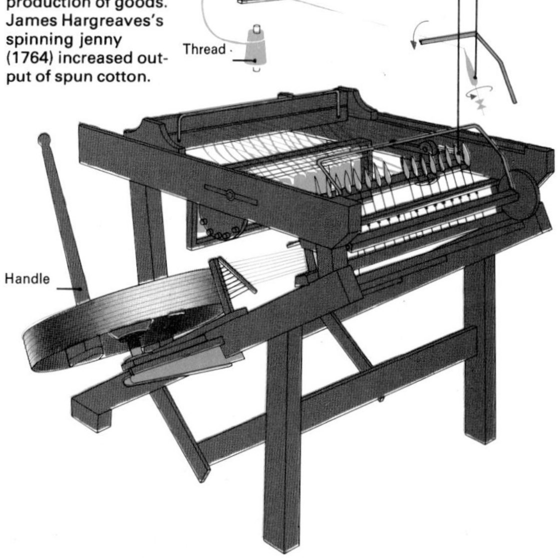

The use of machinery during this period greatly increased the production of goods. James Hargreaves's spinning jenny (1764) increased output of spun cotton.

5

6

7

5 Agriculture could be highly profitable in the later 18th century thanks to a growing population and new techniques, as witness this substantial farmhouse in Gloucestershire. Enclosures grouped fields into more efficient units, permitting the use of four-crop and other rotations while selective breeding and inventions such as Jethro Tull's seed drill contributed to increased agricultural prosperity.

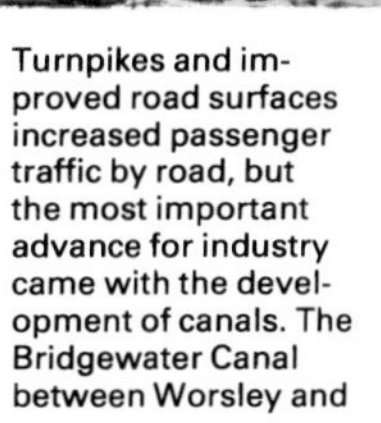

6 Transport developments played a vital part in the Industrial Revolution by widening markets and allowing production to be concentrated where goods could be brought by cheap bulk transport. Turnpikes and improved road surfaces increased passenger traffic by road, but the most important advance for industry came with the development of canals. The Bridgewater Canal between Worsley and Manchester was built for the Duke of Bridgewater by James Brindley (1716–72), an engineer who remained illiterate until his death. The canal, opened in 1761, halved the cost of coal in Manchester by reducing transport costs. In the "canal mania" that followed, an extensive canal network was built up and many early industries were based on it, giving them access to raw materials and markets.

8 Josiah Wedgwood (1730–95) pioneered the large-scale production of pottery at his Etruria works near Stoke-on-Trent. He was a self-educated man and typical of those who made the Industrial Revolution.

9

8

7 A pioneer of the factory system, Sir Richard Arkwright (1732–92) built this cotton mill at Cromford, Derbyshire, which Joseph Wright of Derby painted in the 1780s. The first factories were built for the textile industry, where mechanization and the use first of water power, then of steam, made concentration of production essential. Factories increased in size as steam became the principal source of power. The words "factory" and "mill" were synonymous for a long while.

9 Labour conditions were often poor in the early stages of the Industrial Revolution. Child labour was common, especially in the textile industry, with long hours of work, low pay and frequent accidents. Women also worked in the textile factories, where they made up half the workforce. Though women and children had worked on the land, these new industrial conditions provoked a series of Parliamentary enquiries in Britain and by the mid-19th century Factory Acts were passed, restricting hours of work and prohibiting women and children from certain areas of employment, such as work underground. By 1900 most other industrialized nations had also introduced some form of factory legislation.

Pitt, Fox and the call for reform

The age of the younger William Pitt (1759–1806) and Charles Fox (1749–1806) saw the beginning of the transformation that turned Britain from an agricultural society governed by a narrow oligarchy of the landed classes into an urban, industrial society with democratic rights for most of its inhabitants. During the 60-year reign of George III (reigned 1760–1820), economic and social change greatly enlivened political debate.

Party lines tended to harden during the latter part of the century, replacing the more fluid groupings of the time of Robert Walpole (1676–1745), and reflecting the rise of more divisive issues in politics, such as the American crisis, the power of the Crown, and the Wilkes affair. Out of these were born the demand for parliamentary reform and the emergence, for the first time since 1715, of something approaching a two-party division under the leadership of Pitt and Fox.

The power of the Crown

The accession of George III provoked a period of instability in British politics. The king's dismissal of the existing administration under the elder William Pitt (1708–78) and the Duke of Newcastle (1693–1768) was followed in 1762 by the elevation of the king's favourite, the Earl of Bute (1713–92), to lead the administration. These actions, as well as the pronouncements of the new king, reawakened fears that the Crown would attempt to dominate politics and that the mixed constitution of Crown, Lords and Commons, embodied in the Glorious Revolution of 1689 would be undermined.

In fact, George III was not aiming at the royalist reaction that his opponents feared. An inexperienced and obstinate young king, he wished to free the Crown from the domination of the group of politicians that had held power under George II (reigned 1727–60), especially the elder Pitt. The allegations that the king tyrannized his ministers and controlled a vast web of patronage were much exaggerated.

Nevertheless the resentments of the ousted Whig leaders were articulated in Edmund Burke's *Thoughts on the Cause of the Present Discontents*, published in 1770 [3]. Burke argued that the manipulation of patronage by the Crown permitted the monarch to dominate Parliament and rest his government upon a small group of "King's Friends", thus destroying the independence of the House of Commons.

At the beginning of George III's reign the attempts to exclude the MP John Wilkes (1727–97) [Key] seemed to suggest that the Commons was no longer an independent body or even representative of those who already had the vote.

Demands for reform

Hence the early years of George III's reign saw the rise of demands for reform. These were intended to reduce the influence of the Crown by removing the "rotten" boroughs and giving more seats to the large county electorates and some of the new manufacturing towns. The agitation for reform by the Yorkshire Association under Christopher Wyvill (1740–1822) and by John Wilkes's supporters in Middlesex and the City of London reflected feeling among small landowners and merchants. The war with America aroused still more dissatisfaction.

CONNECTIONS

See also
England under the Hanoverians
The agricultural revolution
Scotland in the 18th century
The British Labour Movement to 1868
The fight for the vote
Ireland from Union to Partition

In other volumes
Europe: economy and society, 1700-1800 (29)
India from the Moguls to 1800 (30)
British colonial policy in the 18th century (30)
The American Revolution (30)

1 William Pitt, 1st Earl of Chatham, was secretary of state from 1756 to 1761 and the foremost politician of his age, known as the "Great Commoner". During his period in power he was absorbed in the Seven Years War (1756–63) and left the management of Parliament and elections to the Duke of Newcastle. Pitt kept free of party ties and showed no interest in parliamentary reform, despite his close friendship with Wilkes. His last political act was to plead for a policy of self-government under the Crown for the American colonies. He formed a second administration in 1766, but ill health forced him to retire from politics in 1768.

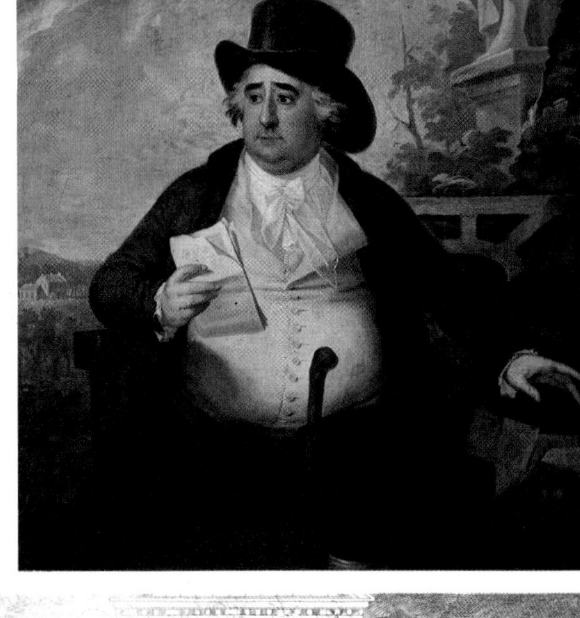

2 Charles James Fox was the effective leader of the Whigs during the last decades of the 18th century. Independent minded, a brilliant orator and a spendthrift who amassed huge gambling debts, Fox is remembered for his vigorous opposition to the Crown and his support for parliamentary reform and the anti-slavery movement. As a party leader he was not very successful, holding office only twice, in 1783 and 1806. His bitter opposition to George III deprived him of royal favour and kept him from power. In addition, his support for the French Revolution split the Whigs and lost him support, as did his opposition to Pitt's repressive acts in the 1790s.

3 Edmund Burke (1729–97) was one of the leading politicians and political philosophers of the 18th century. A Whig, he articulated the theory of "loyal" opposition to the government of the day, blaming the corruption and alleged oligarchic tendencies of George III's reign for political instability and the disorders of the Wilkes affair. He sympathized with the American colonists' struggle for independence from England, but was opposed to the French Revolution for destroying the historically established, traditional institutions of the country. He broke with Fox and the Whigs over this in 1791 and campaigned for war against France until his death in 1797.

4 The Gordon Riots in June 1780 were caused by opposition to the removal of legal penalties from Roman Catholics. In 1779, an extreme Protestant Association was formed by Lord Gordon (1751–93) to prevent what was believed to be growing Catholic power. Petitions and demonstrations were followed by a week of rioting and looting in central London after the Commons refused to debate their cause. Newgate prison was stormed and burned (shown here), property looted and the Bank of England attacked. More than 400 people were killed in the rioting and looting.

Its incompetent handling, leading to defeat, contributed in 1782 to the fall of Lord North's (1732–92) administration, which had held power since 1770.

The re-emergence of two parties

After a confused period with three ministries in under two years, William Pitt formed a government in 1784. Although he never used the word "Tory" himself, Pitt proved, over his long administration, to be the re-founder of the Tory Party. Fox then emerged as the leader of the Whigs and the effective opposition. The early struggles with George III had helped to sharpen party lines and legitimize opposition. Although the Whig and Tory parties were still more fluid than they were to become, Pitt and Fox provided leadership to a more coherent grouping of supporters than had been the case earlier in the century.

The passing of the "economical reform" acts in 1782 – reducing the number of officers in the pay of the Crown eligible to sit in Parliament – contributed to the waning of royal influence. The professionalization of the civil service under Pitt and his drive for greater economy further reduced offices and sinecures. George III's recurrent breakdowns into insanity contributed to the decline of monarchical power, culminating in his permanent incapacity in the last ten years of his life. Even so, the king retained sufficient personal influence to exclude Fox from office for much of the period and to support Pitt's administration. It was the king's obstinacy over Catholic emancipation that forced Pitt's resignation in 1801.

The last years of Pitt and Fox were dominated by the impact of the French Revolution and the wars with France. Pitt was forced to act against the threat of subversion in England with a series of repressive measures, culminating in the treason trials of 1794 – aimed at the radical Corresponding Societies – and the Two Acts of 1795. During those years, Fox alienated many of his parliamentary supporters by his support of the French Revolution at a time when its excesses shocked the majority of propertied opinion. Nonetheless, his opposition to the policies of Pitt and his brilliant oratory preserved the Whig's image as the party of reform.

John Wilkes achieved notoriety as one of the early champions of reform after he was arrested for criticizing George III in his *North Briton* newspaper, in 1763. Wilkes claimed immunity as an MP, but he was expelled from the House of Commons. In 1768 Wilkes was elected MP for Middlesex. He became a focus for popular discontent with the Government and was able to manipulate this to cause riots in London in 1768. Imprisoned, Wilkes was re-elected three times, each time being expelled by the Commons. In 1774 he was finally allowed to take his seat in the House, but his assertion of popular opinion and freedom in politics was not forgotten.

5

5 Poor harvests and high prices caused several waves of food riots in the late 18th and early 19th centuries. In particular, the wars with France from 1793 led to great hardship and many popular disturbances. In 1800, the price of corn was more than treble the price in 1790.

6

6 William Pitt, the Younger who led the Tory Party from 1784, is shown here dominating the House of Commons. He held office with only a short break, from 1801–04, until his death. His inexperience led to early defeats of his attempts to reform Parliament and create a police force for London, but he soon established a stable and efficient administration. Pitt reduced patronage and reorganized the civil service, while settling colonial affairs in India with his India Act of 1784. As a war minister after 1793, he was not totally successful. Taxation and defeats abroad made his Government unpopular, but he weathered the crisis, introducing repressive measures against the radical societies at home. In 1801, he resigned over the king's opposition to Catholic emancipation, but returned as prime minister in 1804 for two troubled years before his death.

7

7 The movement for parliamentary reform gathered momentum in the last 25 years of the 18th century. This cartoon shows reformers attacking the "rotten" boroughs, the virtually uninhabited towns that still elected members to Parliament. Old Sarum was a notorious example of this – there a handful of voters returned two MPs. In addition, many seats were at the disposal of landed patrons, the so-called "pocket" boroughs. The larger manufacturing towns such as Manchester, Sheffield, Birmingham and Leeds were unrepresented, and the voting qualifications varied from town to town. The younger Pitt introduced a bill in 1785 to remove some of the rotten boroughs, but it was defeated in the Commons.

8

8 Agitation for reform culminated in the Reform Bill struggle of 1830–32. The Whig Government was returned in 1830 pledged to carry a reform bill. But rejection of the bill by the Lords in 1831 precipitated severe rioting in many parts of the country. At Bristol there were four days of riots and in Nottingham the castle was burnt (shown here) by supporters of the bill. The bill was finally passed in 1832.

Nelson and Wellington

For many centuries Britain opposed any European power that threatened to dominate continental Europe and from 1793 to 1814, with a short break in 1801–2, it fought to defeat the spreading power of revolutionary France. Lacking a large army, Britain had to rely on the traditional strategy of organizing alliances of other continental powers while using its naval supremacy to weaken France by blockade. Whenever possible, troops were sent to help anti-French forces, but Britain's major contributions to the ultimate defeat of France were a willingness to continue fighting, alone if necessary until new allies were found, and the use of a long-established prowess at sea.

Britain's weapons

The Royal Navy had long been recognized as the bulwark of British security but conditions of service were grim. The numbers of recruits needed to man the wartime fleet could only be maintained by forcible impressment [1] and the recruitment of convicts. Once enlisted, men were rarely allowed to leave.

In contrast to the conscript armies of Europe, the British army at that time was a small volunteer force numbered in tens, rather than hundreds, of thousands. Officers were able to buy their commissions, received no professional training and usually paid scant attention to the welfare of their men. By the end of the eighteenth century, however, efforts were being made to organize supply and medical services [2].

Nelson's great triumphs

Throughout the Napoleonic Wars Britain was fortunate to be served by a number of exceptional naval officers who proved to be both fine seamen and outstanding leaders. The greatest of these was Horatio Nelson (1758–1805).

At the outbreak of war Nelson commanded a ship-of-the-line in the Mediterranean and acquired a reputation as an active, able officer. During the Battle of St Vincent on 14 February 1797 his initiative in breaking the line of battle led to the capture of four enemy ships. For his part in the victory Nelson was knighted and promoted to rear-admiral. Wounded in several engagements, he lost an eye and an arm but his mental powers remained undiminished. In 1798, when Napoleon attempted to cut Britain off from India and its other eastern possessions by invading Egypt, Nelson annihilated the French fleet in the Battle of the Nile, fought in Aboukir Bay. Of the 17 French ships, 13 were captured or destroyed.

The victor of the Nile, now created Baron Nelson of the Nile, took command of the Mediterranean fleet in 1803. For the next two years, in a remarkable display of seamanship, Nelson off Toulon and Admiral William Cornwallis (1744–1819) off Brest kept the French fleet immobile. In 1805 the Toulon force managed to slip out and head for the West Indies meaning to return, link up with other forces and establish temporary command of the Channel so that Napoleon could invade Britain. But the French were forced into Cadiz while the British gathered outside under Nelson's command off the Cape of Trafalgar. When the combined French and Spanish fleet emerged it was utterly destroyed in battle [5] on 21 October 1805. Although Nelson was killed on the quarter-

CONNECTIONS

See also
Pitt, Fox and the call for reform
British foreign policy 1815-1914

In other volumes
The French Revolution (29)
Napoleonic Europe (29)
The Congress of Vienna (29)

1 The hated press-gangs, armed with cudgels, terrorized towns as they went ashore and roamed the streets in search of able-bodied men for the navy. Victims were forcibly seized and dragged aboard for medical examination. Volunteers were few, for life at sea meant separation from their wives and families for long periods, bad food, wretched conditions and brutal discipline; yet morale under Nelson was high.

2 Women were considered to be more a hindrance than a help in the army of Wellington's day, as implied in this drawing by Thomas Rowlandson. Some wives, but not many, were allowed to accompany their husbands on a campaign: the number was limited to between 2 and 6 per company of 100. Those women who did go received half-rations free. Some even took children as well. The women cooked meals, did soldiers' washing and acted as nurses. They had an eye for booty, too. Wellington once observed that "The women are at least as bad, if not worse, than the men as plunderers".

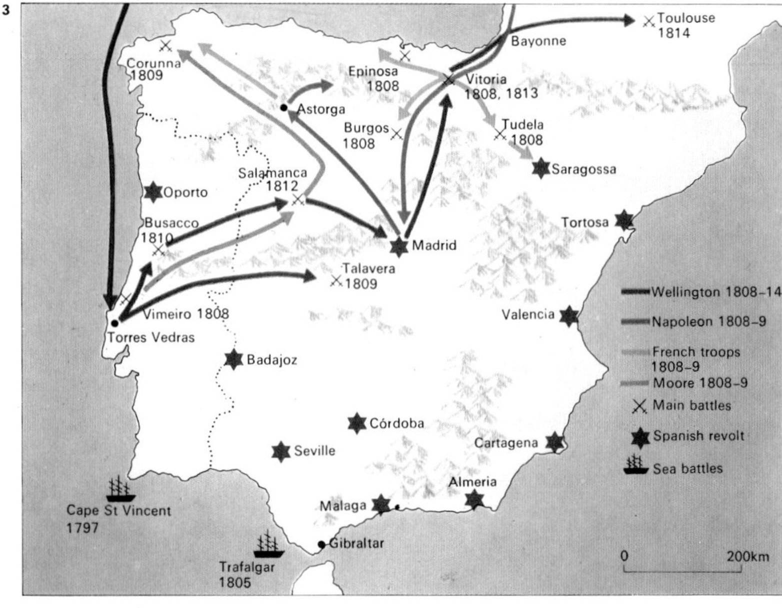

3 The French took Spain swiftly and compelled the British to leave. After Oporto fell (1807) Portugal appealed to Britain for aid and Wellington sailed with a force of 17,000. Napoleon ordered his commanders to drive the British into the sea, but the French themselves were expelled from the Peninsula and sent scurrying across their own border, with Wellington in pursuit. Napoleon later said that the "Spanish ulcer", with constant guerrilla activity and rioting, undermined his empire.

4 HMS *Victory*, Nelson's flagship at Trafalgar, was typical of the ships-of-the-line that formed the main battle fleet. Floating batteries with 60 to 120 guns firing in broadsides and a complement of 700, these slow, unwieldy vessels could remain at sea for years on end. Built at Chatham, and launched in 1765, Victory was 69.5m long with a beam of 15.5m. She had more than 100 guns, the largest of which were two 68-pounders, 30 32-pounders and 28 24-pounders.

deck of HMS *Victory* [4] at the height of the engagement [6], he died knowing he had won a decisive victory.

The road to Waterloo

Nelson's success ended any hopes Napoleon had of invading Britain. The French emperor was therefore forced to try to destroy Britain by closing Europe to British trade. When Portugal and Spain refused to join the blockade, the French invaded. Britain was thus given the opportunity to intervene militarily. An expedition to Spain under John Moore (1761–1809) was compelled to retire but in August 1808 a second force under Sir Arthur Wellesley (1769–1852) [Key], later Duke of Wellington, landed in Portugal.

An Anglo-Irish aristocrat, Wellington learnt his soldiering skills in India from 1796 to 1805. After taking part in unsuccessful expeditions in north-western Europe in 1806 and 1807 he was given command in the Peninsula. There for the next three years he showed great skill in tying down vastly superior French forces [3]. He was always prepared to withdraw behind defences when necessary, but emerged to inflict a succession of defeats on the French. Finally in 1811 he launched a major offensive that cleared the Peninsula, winning major victories at Salamanca and Vittoria before invading south-west France in 1814 [7].

Napoleon abdicated and left for exile in Elba, but almost a year later he returned to France in an attempt to regain the throne. To meet this renewed threat Britain and the allies – Austria, Prussia and Russia – appointed Wellington to command a combined army gathered in Belgium. Despite being surprised by the speed of Napoleon's opening manoeuvres, Wellington held his ground against superior forces near the village of Waterloo [8] until Marshal Gebhard von Blücher (1742-1819) and a Prussian army arrived and completed a crushing victory.

For the second time Napoleon abdicated and went into exile – this time to St Helena, until his death in 1821. The victories of Nelson and Wellington, coupled with the nation's industrial and commercial supremacy, now made Britain the most powerful nation in the world.

KEY

"A Wellington Boot, or the Head of the Army": this 1827 cartoon shows the Iron Duke's distinctive profile and characteristic footwear. Taciturn and aloof, he affected to despise the troops he commanded as the "scum of the earth" but he based his tactics on their steadiness under fire. He chose defensive positions and relied on the discipline of his men to break the massive infantry and cavalry assaults of the French which had shattered most other adversaries. He hid an emotional nature under an icy manner and he cared for the welfare of his men. They repaid him with their respect and by beating the finest troops of Napoleon's *Grande Armée*.

5

5 At Trafalgar the British fleet went into action in two columns. Realizing that he was outnumbered 27 to 33, Nelson eschewed traditional tactics of the single line of battle, and succeeded brilliantly, capturing 19 enemy vessels.

6

6 Nelson's death overshadowed the triumph of Trafalgar. Hit on the shoulder by a musket-ball from a sniper, he was taken below decks where he died four hours later. A stern disciplinarian and a born leader, he displayed in battle great bravery and daring, tactical genius and shrewd judgment. His devotion to duty was absolute and the men he led revered him.

7

7 Wellington had a great welcome when he rode into Toulouse on 12 April 1814. The battle, he said, had been "very severe": combined deaths were 7,700. Victory, however, seemed complete when he learnt later that day that Napoleon had abdicated.

8

8 The Battle of Waterloo (1815) made Wellington a national hero. Napoleon had crossed into Belgium on 15 June and thrust back the Prussian army at Ligny but failed to rout them. Then on the morning of Sunday 18 June he attacked Wellington at Waterloo. Wellington had 67,000 men with 150 guns, Napoleon had 72,000 with 250 guns. The battle soon became a pounding match with few manoeuvres, but the arrival of the Prussians in the early evening brought swift and total victory.

The British Labour Movement to 1868

Craft organizations had existed for centuries in Britain, usually protected by a framework of paternalistic legislation that determined terms of apprenticeship and wages. With the growth of towns and industry during the Industrial Revolution in the eighteenth century, the old craft regulations came under pressure from employers who sought to free industry from rigid restrictions and to introduce labour-saving machinery.

Unrest and the Combination Laws

The wars with revolutionary France, which opened in 1793, were marked by high prices and labour unrest. Fearing the growth of radical ideas among the lower classes, the government passed the Combination Laws of 1799–1800 [Key]. These were the culmination of a series of laws against "combinations" in specific trades. The Combination Laws prohibited any association between two or more workmen to gain either an increase in wages or a decrease in hours. Unions were forced to operate in secret or under the guise of "non-political" Friendly Societies, which were recognized as legal in 1793.

The economic warfare between Britain and France in the latter part of the Napoleonic Wars brought trade depression and hardship to the growing industrial areas. In 1810–12 there occurred the most serious wave of Luddite disturbances [3], in which workmen under a mythical leader, "King Ludd", destroyed machinery which they saw as threatening their livelihood.

This violence was in large part the traditional reaction of workmen threatened with a decline in their living standards. The degree of union organization in the Luddite outbreaks is obscure, but some elements of union organization were undoubtedly present in Nottinghamshire. Further outbreaks of machine-breaking in 1816–17 and 1826 were also firmly repressed.

In the post-war years, continued distress and radical agitation for parliamentary reform made the government suspicious of trade union activities. Strikes in the factory districts took place in spite of the Combination Laws, most notably in Lancashire where the cotton spinners and weavers conducted an extensive strike in 1818. Elsewhere brickmakers and carpenters secured wage advances without being prosecuted.

Postwar agitation came to a climax in the St Peter's Fields meeting in Manchester of August 1819 [5]. The Peterloo Massacre, as it was dubbed by the radical press, helped to create a more sympathetic attitude towards working-class organizations. The writings of men such as William Cobbett (1763–1835) [4] were also creating a more self-conscious desire for improvement among workmen.

Growth in union membership

In the easier economic climate after 1820, the Combination Laws were attacked. A former tailor, Francis Place (1771–1854), devoted himself to the legalization of trade unions and, with the support of radical MPs, secured the repeal of the Combination Laws in 1824. Unions could now bargain about conditions although still surrounded by some restrictions. Attempts, in 1830 and 1833 to form a single national union failed. Many unions turned to "new model unionism", emphasizing their respectability and rejecting militant activity.

CONNECTIONS

See also
The agricultural revolution
Scotland in the 18th century
Pitt, Fox and the call for reform
Social reform 1800-1914
Victoria and her statesmen
The fight for the vote
Scotland in the 19th century
The British Labour Movement 1868-1930

In other volumes
Political thought in the 19th century (29)
Early socialism in the West (29)
The American Revolution (30)

1 Thomas Paine's (1737–1809) *The Rights of Man* (1791–2) was published in reply to Edmund Burke's (1729–97) criticisms of the French Revolution. It did much to stimulate popular radicalism. However, threat of prosecution forced Paine to flee the country for France in September 1792.

2 Disturbances broke out in England between 1830 and 1832 in which agricultural labourers protested against unemployment, low wages and the introduction of threshing machines. The unrest was not politically motivated, but was a reaction to growing poverty. Nine labourers were hanged and 457 transported.

3 Luddite rioters of 1810–12 and 1816–17 smashed factory machinery in protest against the introduction of new equipment in the hosiery and woollen cloth industries. The protesters claimed to be led by a "Ned" or "King Ludd" whose name was attached to public letters denouncing the introduction of the new machinery. The riots caused a series of harsh measures to be enacted by the government.

4 William Cobbett was the most influential of the radical critics and writers in the parliamentary reform movement. Of humble origin, he published a number of radical newspapers including, in 1816, the weekly *Political Register*, which soon had an estimated sale of 60,000 copies a week among working men. His hatred of the new industrialism is evident in his documentary *Rural Rides* (1830).

5 The Peterloo Massacre, so-called, was a tragic fracas that took place in August 1819. Manchester reformers called a meeting at which the radical demagogue "Orator" Henry Hunt (1773–1835) was to speak. But the local magistrates, fearing trouble, ordered the yeomanry to arrest Hunt at the meeting. When this failed, Hussars were sent in against the crowd of 60,000, and in the ensuing confusion 11 people were killed and more than 400 injured, including women and children. The incident was used by the government as a pretext for introducing a fresh wave of repressive legislation, the Six Acts, against "seditious assemblies" and politically "subversive" literature.

By the 1840s most unions consisted of skilled workmen and the bulk of semi- and unskilled workers still lay outside union organization. The conviction of the "Tolpuddle Martyrs" in Dorset in 1834 [6] for administering unlawful oaths showed the obstacles that could still face unskilled workers who tried to organize themselves.

Many unions took an ambivalent attitude towards the Chartist demands for the vote contained in the People's Charter [7]. Elite craft groups, such as the engineers or potters, were reluctant to align themselves with a movement tainted with violence and disorder. Some of the declining crafts, however, such as the handloom weavers, participated in Chartism as a desperate attempt to reverse their deteriorating situation.

With the decline of Chartism after 1848, the craft unions continued to consolidate their position. By 1852, the Amalgamated Society of Engineers had 12,000 members, centralized control, and high rates of subscription, which enabled it to wage successful strikes. Unskilled workers formed organizations, such as the Miners' Association of 1842, but still lacked the solidarity and strength of the skilled workmen.

From the period of model unionism, there was an improvement in the public image of the trade union movement. The Friendly Societies and Co-operative Movement, founded at Rochdale in 1844, were aided by middle-class sympathizers [9].

Co-ordination of union activities

In 1866–7, a short trade slump in the midst of improving conditions led to a number of strikes and some violence, notably at Sheffield. The "Sheffield Outrages" [10] led to a Royal Commission in 1867 on trade unions. The Commission recommended putting trade unions upon a firm legal basis and allowing them to secure their funds. These gains were established in the Trades Union Act of 1871. In 1868 the Trades Union Congress (TUC) was founded in Manchester with 34 delegates. In 1869 in Birmingham, quarter of a million trade unionists were represented at the TUC by 40 delegates and a "Parliamentary Committee" was established to represent trade union interests.

Repressive measures were adopted by the government against radical societies which arose following the French Revolution. Habeas corpus was suspended in May 1794, and some radical leaders were charged with high treason. In 1795, following an attack upon the king's coach in October, the Two Acts were passed. These restricted the right of free assembly and extended the law of treason to cover acts of speech and writing. The laws against combinations restricted the growth of trade unions. After 1815 the government again resorted to laws against meetings and radical propaganda, in the "gagging" Acts of 1817 and the Six Acts of 1819.

6 The precarious legal status of early trade unions was illustrated when six Dorset labourers were arrested in 1834 for swearing men into a union at the village of Tolpuddle. All were sentenced to seven years transportation. After demonstrations such as this, they were pardoned in 1836.

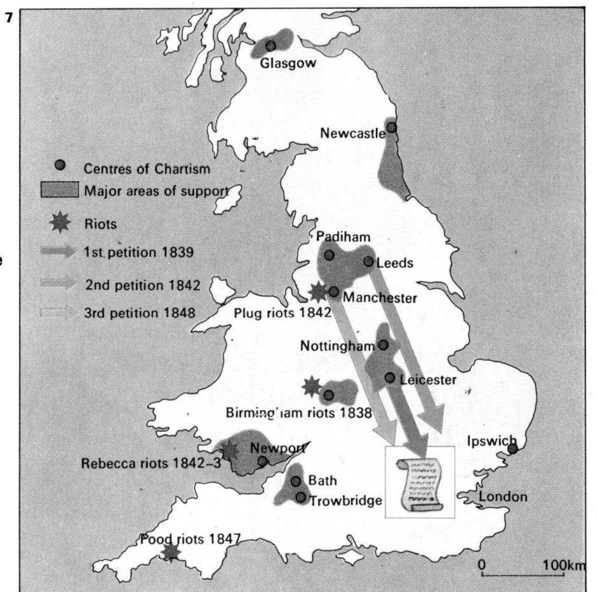

7 Chartism, expressed in the People's Charter, owed its origins to the failure of the 1832 bill fully to enfranchise the working man. The Charter demanded male suffrage, secret ballot, annual parliaments, equal electoral districts, an end to property qualifications for MPs and the introduction of official payment for them.

8 The Anti-Corn Law League, which was mainly composed of industrialists, was founded in 1839 to oppose the duties on imported corn that protected domestic producers. Although the League was campaigning for cheaper food in opposition to the power of the landed classes, the Chartists and the working classes did not fully support it. The Chartists argued that in reality the League wanted wages reduced by the amount that corn prices would fall if the Laws were repealed.

9 The first Co-operative shop, a non-profit making retail store, was one of a number of co-operative ventures in the 1830s and 1840s. By selling cheap and pure food it was the most successful.

10 The "Sheffield Outrages", a series of violent incidents directed at non-union members, led to the establishment of a Royal Commission to investigate the status of trade unions. In 1867 union status was further put into question by a ruling that they were defenceless against officials who absconded with union funds. Unions were represented on the Commission which recommended that they be given a legal basis.

THE SHEFFIELD HEROES.

Mr R...... PITY THE SORROWS OF A POOR OLD MAN.

WORKMAN. IT'S NO USE OLD BOY, WE'RE NOT TO BE CAUGHT WITH CHAFF, YOU'VE DECEIVED US LONG ENOUGH, MUNDELLA IS THE MAN OF OUR CHOICE.

No6

Social reform 1800-1914

The rapid increase in population and new industrial towns during the Industrial Revolution created immense social problems in Britain. The new towns had grown uncontrolled, many lacked basic amenities such as sanitation and water supply, and the problems of poverty, ill-health, crime and bad housing were widespread. There was almost no schooling for most of the population. Child and female labour was regularly used in factories and mines [1], even for the most arduous and dangerous tasks. The prevailing ethic of laissez-faire that the state should not interfere with the workings of the economy or society held back any far-reaching legislation to improve working conditions.

Poverty and social concern

During the course of the nineteenth century some of these evils were diagnosed and brought to public notice by social commentators [8] and novelists such as Charles Dickens (1812–70), Mrs Gaskell (1810–65) and Charles Kingsley (1819–75). In addition, parliamentary enquiries were set up to examine social questions. The result was a considerable body of social legislation.

The Poor Law was a source of concern to nineteenth-century reformers. The existing system of "outdoor" relief, levied from parish rates, burdened the propertied classes, and Thomas Malthus (1766–1834) in his influential *Essay on the Principle of Population* (1798) had argued that it perpetuated poverty by encouraging population growth. Under the Speenhamland system, introduced in 1795, labourers' wages were subsidized out of parochial funds on a scale linked to the price of bread. But in the large industrial towns, the parochial organization of poor relief was totally inadequate to meet the strains of heavy unemployment.

In 1834 the New Poor Law was passed. It much reduced "outdoor relief". Instead of receiving charity, all able-bodied people requiring relief were forced to go into the workhouse, where a strict regime, including segregation of the sexes, even of married couples, was intended to deter all but the truly destitute [5]. In addition, poor law authorities were amalgamated to spread the burden of poor relief evenly.

The insanitary conditions of the great towns gave rise to considerable concern about public health. In the 1840s an inquiry showed that more than half the major towns in Britain had an insufficient or impure water supply. The cholera epidemics of the mid-nineteenth century acted as a spur to the public health movement. Edwin Chadwick's (1800–90) famous *Report on the Sanitary Conditions of the Labouring Population* in 1842 led to the creation of a central Board of Health under the Public Health Act of 1848. Individual towns were empowered to set up local Medical Officers of Health. In 1875 a Public Health Act laid the foundations for an overhaul of public sanitation.

Legislation on housing

Housing reform was left to piecemeal action. Lord Shaftesbury's (1801–85) [2] Lodging Houses Act of 1851 checked the worst abuses of "doss-houses". More important, however, was the Artisans' Dwelling Act of 1875 which gave local authorities the power to clear slums. A number of reforms of local government, especially the Municipal

CONNECTIONS

See also
The British Labour Movement to 1868
Victorian London
The fight for the vote

In other volumes
The Industrial Revolution (29)
Industrialization 1870-1914 (31)
The novel and the press in the 19th century (34)

1 The use of child and female labour in factories and mines during the Industrial Revolution was widespread. In the early 1830s, nearly half the labour force in the cotton mills was under 21, and of the adults more than half were women. Hours and conditions were regulated only by the benevolence of employers, and a working week exceeding 90 hours was common until the 1833 Factory Act became effective.

2 Lord Shaftesbury was an evangelical churchman and a dedicated reformer. He is associated with the 1833 Factory Act and with legislation to prohibit the employment of children by chimney sweeps, in 1840, and of women and children in the mines, in 1842. But his overriding paternalism made him unsympathetic to franchise extension in 1867 and to too much state involvement in welfare.

3 The Corn Laws of 1815 protected British agriculture by prohibiting the importation of foreign wheat until the domestic price exceeded 80 shillings per quarter. These laws were widely opposed by the urban poor and also by the industrialists because it was generally thought that they forced up the price of food and wages. In the long term too, it was argued that protectionism would harm exports. In 1839, the Anti-Corn Law League was founded by Richard Cobden (1804–65) and John Bright (1811–89) to agitate for repeal. In attacking the privilege and sectional interests behind the laws, the league took on a reformist appearance. The Corn Laws were repealed in 1846.

4 No free public libraries existed before 1845. From the mid-century, however, many towns set up rate-assisted public libraries to provide access to books and newspapers for all classes.

5 Under the New Poor Law of 1834, workhouse conditions were to be made inferior to those of the poorest labourer outside, in order effectively to deter "laziness" and "vagrancy" among the poor.

Corporations Act of 1835 and the Local Government Act of 1888, provided the administrative machinery necessary to implement these measures on a local level.

Factory legislation began as early as 1802 when Robert Peel senior (1750–1830), introduced an act to limit the employment of children to under 12 hours a day. The 1819 Factory Act forbade the employment of children in cotton mills under the age of nine. Lord Shaftesbury's 1833 Factory Act further limited the working hours of all children under 18 years old and appointed factory inspectors to enforce this. Safety regulations and limitations on women's working hours were introduced by an act in 1844. This legislation was extended in the course of latter part of the nineteenth century to include all types of factories. In 1891, a consolidating act raised the minimum age for the employment of children to 11 years.

The rise of state education

Education remained a patchwork of private initiative and philanthropic effort for much of the nineteenth century. The Royal Lancasterian Association (1810) and the Anglican National Society (1811) founded hundreds of schools without any government involvement. State intervention began in the 1830s and the first government grant to education was made in 1833. In 1839 an education department was set up to inspect grant-receiving schools [6].

In 1870, Forster's Education Act provided virtually free elementary education for anyone who wanted it by setting up local boards empowered to establish schools financed, in part, from the rates. Education up to the age of ten years was made compulsory in 1880. In 1902, the Balfour Education Act created Local Education Authorities and thoroughly reformed the whole system of secondary education.

The growth of state responsibility for social welfare was embodied in the legislation of the Liberal governments after 1906, which went a considerable way towards creating a rudimentary "welfare state", with important, new measures such as the Old Age Pensions Act of 1908 and the National Health Insurance Act of 1911 [10].

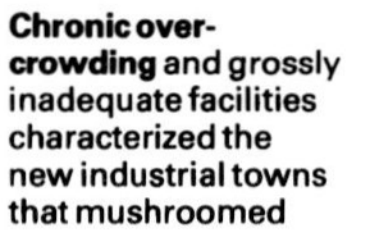

Chronic overcrowding and grossly inadequate facilities characterized the new industrial towns that mushroomed during the Industrial Revolution. The sheer scale and complexity of the problems were quite unprecedented, and unnoticed until social reformers, philanthropists and the unavoidable pressure of events forced them upon public notice.

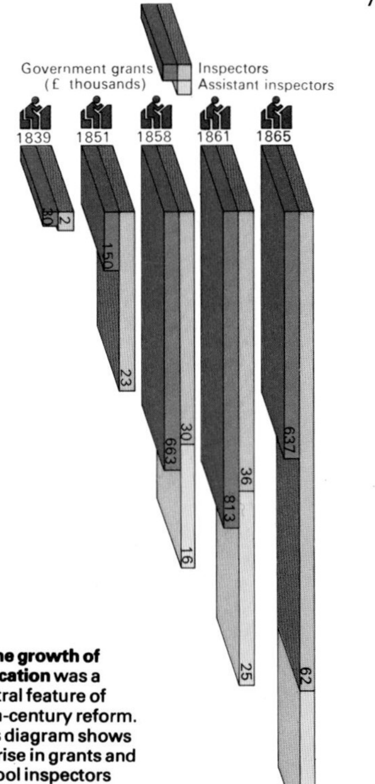

6 The growth of education was a central feature of 19th-century reform. This diagram shows the rise in grants and school inspectors in elementary education between 1839 and 1865.

7 The Salvation Army, founded by "General" William Booth (1829–1912) in 1865, aimed at social as well as spiritual welfare. It provided soup kitchens, night shelters and many facilities for the destitute. Booth was particularly concerned at the adverse effects of urbanisation and the depopulation of the countryside. He hoped that through a system of rural re-education he could reverse this trend.

8 John Ruskin (1819–1900) art critic and reformer argued that art, ethics and social conditions were inextricably linked. Many of his proposals, such as pensions and state education, were later adopted.

10 The National Insurance Act of 1911 provided unemployment pay and free medical treatment in return for graduated weekly contributions to be paid by employers, employees and the state.

9 Private philanthropy in the 19th century very often preceded state action by many years. Port Sunlight, shown here, was built by the industrialist Lord Leverhulme (1851–1925) in 1888. It was the first village to be built on the garden city principles, then advocated as a means to eliminate the physical and moral effects of urban overcrowding by Ruskin and other social reformers. This is shown in the planned houses, open spaces, and the provision of public amenities.

Victoria and her statesmen

Queen Victoria's (1819-1901) reign, from 1837 to 1901, lasted longer than that of any other British monarch. During that time the party system and parliamentary democracy came to their maturity. The monarchy moved out of active politics, but achieved a new status as the neutral guardian of national stability. In 1830 even *The Times* had found it difficult to mourn the death of George IV; republicanism was a serious radical cry. By 1897, the year of the Diamond Jubilee [9], republicanism had been drowned in popular royalist enthusiasm.

The changing style of politics

Ten prime ministers served Queen Victoria [Key]. None of them was chosen by her in defiance of the wishes of the Commons. Each came to power by virtue of being the leader of his party, and cabinets were composed of members of the same party. That was a marked though gradual change from the eighteenth-century politics of connection. Party had replaced the Crown as the source of political power. After the 1832 Reform Act, both the Whigs and the Conservatives took steps to organize themselves into national parties. Elections lost much local colour and acquired national meaning.

The first half of the reign

It was not easy for the 18-year-old princess to step with confidence onto the crowded political stage. Victoria was fortunate to find a devoted tutor in her first prime minister, Lord Melbourne (William Lamb) (1779-1848), then mellowed with age. His marriage to Lady Caroline Ponsonby, marked by her brief affair with the poet Byron, had ended in 1825, and the young Victoria formed a close friendship with him, as with a father.

She was loath to part with Melbourne. But the weakness of her constitutional position was brought home to her by the Conservative victory at the 1841 elections. Loving Melbourne, she had learned to love the Whigs. Losing him, she learned to work as closely and fairly with his successor. Throughout her reign she kept herself fully informed on political developments; her opinions could never be treated lightly by her ministers.

Robert Peel, from 1841 to 1846 the first prime minister of a Conservative (as opposed to a purely Tory) Party, was a new breed of prime minister. His roots were commercial and his forte was economics. He had no sentimental attachment to the landed aristocracy. The squires on the backbenches, the heart of his party, found him uncommunicative and arrogant. He tried to turn the Tories into a party that worked to balance the claims of competing interests [1], instead of seeking to defend the exclusive interests of the land and the Church. He failed, split his party, and left it a minority for a generation.

Viscount Palmerston (1784–1865) was the beneficiary of this Conservative misfortune. He was prime minister for all but 14 months between 1855 and 1865. England was then enjoying the mid-Victorian boom; the standard of living was generally high and social problems unobtrusive. Palmerston believed that a government did best by doing as little as possible. His great interest was foreign affairs, the one sphere where the royal will still counted for something. He

CONNECTIONS

See also
Pitt, Fox and the call for reform
Social reform 1800-1914
Victorian London
Ireland from Union to Partition
British foreign policy 1815-1914

In other volumes
The British Empire in the 19th century (31)

1 Robert Peel (1788–1850) sought an undoctrinaire approach to the problems of industrialization that brought violent Chartist unrest, and in 1846 after the Irish famine he alienated the traditionally Tory landowners by removing tariffs on imported corn, thus reducing the price of bread.

2 The Great Exhibition (1851) at the Crystal Palace, asserted Victoria's international standing early in her reign. Rulers from many parts of the world attended the festivities, which were originally conceived by Prince Albert to celebrate the wonders of industry and to promote peace.

3 Prince Albert (1819–61), married Victoria in 1840, and rebuilt much of the Kensington district of London for the Great Exhibition. Among the monuments erected to him was the Albert Bridge, shown here.

4 Disraeli became Conservative leader in the Commons in 1849. He passed the 1867 Reform Act in an attempt to outbid the Liberals for popular appeal, and founded the Conservative Central Office (1868) to organize the party in the country.

and Victoria clashed often and she sometimes won. In 1857 Palmerston made light of the Indian Mutiny; Victoria knew better, and it was on her initiative that troop reinforcements were sent to India which saved the British presence there.

Gladstone and Disraeli

Palmerston's death in 1865 allowed William Ewart Gladstone (1809–98) [6] to assume the leadership of the Liberal Party. He was the first prime minister to form four governments (1868–74, 1880–85, 1886, 1892–4). He was too single-minded, too earnest, and too radical to earn anything but Victoria's habitual distrust. But he was beyond question the giant of Victorian politicians. Under his premiership the Irish Church was disestablished (1869), secondary education made universal (1870), the secret ballot introduced (1872), and the agricultural labourer enfranchised (1884). His mission, he said, was to pacify Ireland, but his Home Rule Bill of 1886 was defeated by Liberal Unionists, led by Joseph Chamberlain (1836–1914), perhaps the greatest Victorian statesman never to be prime minister.

Gladstone's great rival was Benjamin Disraeli (1804–81) [4], already a tired man at the start of his main ministry (1874–80). His achievement was to help swell the tide of imperial sentiment by his rhetoric and, by making Victoria Empress of India in 1876, to exalt in the popular imagination the person and office of the monarch. And she for six years found in "Dizzy" an unfailingly courteous and amusing companion. He was her favourite prime minister. It was an extraordinary end to the career of one who, from his Jewish descent, his landless status, and suspect literary connections, had never become quite acceptable even to his own Conservative party.

His successor as Conservative leader, Lord Salisbury (1830–1903) [7], was in the purest Tory mould, the last great representative of the Cecil family that had risen to prominence under Elizabeth I. He was the ideal minister to preside over the Jubilee celebrations. He formed three administrations (1885–6, 1886–92, 1895–1902), and left politics just after the queen's death.

KEY

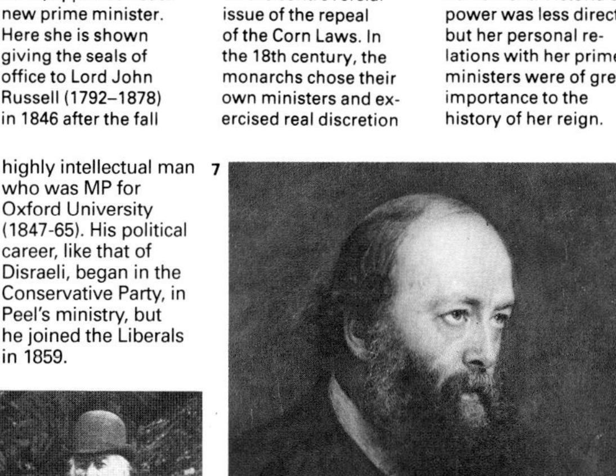

The queen, as head of state, appointed each new prime minister. Here she is shown giving the seals of office to Lord John Russell (1792–1878) in 1846 after the fall of Peel's ministry on the controversial issue of the repeal of the Corn Laws. In the 18th century, the monarchs chose their own ministers and exercised real discretion over dissolutions of Parliament. Victoria's power was less direct but her personal relations with her prime ministers were of great importance to the history of her reign.

5

5 The death of Albert in 1861 led Victoria to withdraw from social life and dress in mourning for many years. At this point her popularity reached its lowest ebb, but revived by the 1880s. She never recovered from the loss of her German-born husband.

6 Gladstone was the son of a Liverpool cotton merchant and retained a radical and evangelical outlook throughout his career. His stirring oratory made him the darling of the industrial masses, but he was a highly intellectual man who was MP for Oxford University (1847-65). His political career, like that of Disraeli, began in the Conservative Party, in Peel's ministry, but he joined the Liberals in 1859.

6

7

7 Lord Salisbury was enigmatic and shy and an implacable foe of Irish Home Rule. He made the Conservative Party into the most powerful party in the state by 1902.

8

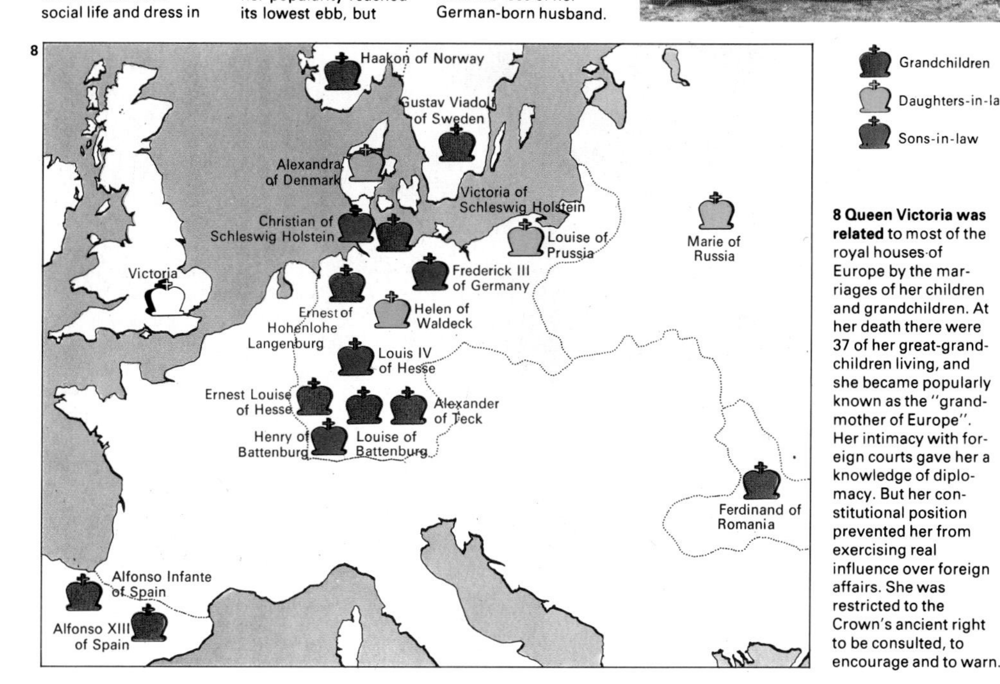

8 Queen Victoria was related to most of the royal houses of Europe by the marriages of her children and grandchildren. At her death there were 37 of her great-grandchildren living, and she became popularly known as the "grandmother of Europe". Her intimacy with foreign courts gave her a knowledge of diplomacy. But her constitutional position prevented her from exercising real influence over foreign affairs. She was restricted to the Crown's ancient right to be consulted, to encourage and to warn.

9

9 The Diamond Jubilee of 22 June 1897 was a grand imperial festival which was attended by representatives of Victoria's 387 million subjects. The queen was 78 and suffered from rheumatism and failing eyesight. The short service at St Paul's, which marked the halfway point of the royal procession from Buckingham Palace, was held outside the cathedral to avoid carrying the queen up the steps in a wheelchair. Like the jubilee of 1887 the Diamond Jubilee provided an occasion for a colonial conference.

Victorian London

In the nineteenth century, London became the biggest and richest city in the world, its population quadrupling to reach 6,586,269 by 1901 in Greater London (a term first used in the 1881 census). Its growth as the heart of a great commercial and military empire presented a spectacle both imposing and appalling. Between the plush and cut-glass elegance of the West End and the fever-ridden slums of Dickensian description lay a gulf the century could not bridge. Overwhelmed by the squalor in which many of the people lived, the critic John Ruskin in 1865 called London "rattling, growling, smoking, stinking – a ghastly heap of fermenting brickwork pouring out poison at every pore".

Commerical expansion

The port of London was central to the economic growth of the capital. The first large enclosed docks were completed in 1802. In 1885 the expansion of trade was marked by the completion of the Victoria Dock, which measured two kilometres. Although challenged by ports such as Hull and Liverpool, London remained the premier port, and 13 million tonnes of goods passed through it in 1880.

London was the centre of a host of industries associated with trade, refining and processing imported goods for distribution to the rest of the country or for re-export. In addition to brewing, distilling, tanning and food-processing the capital supported a shipbuilding industry that was overtaken by Newcastle and Glasgow only in the closing years of the century. By 1851 there were almost half a million workers engaged in manufacturing. Service industries employed nearly one million by 1861.

Even before the end of the eighteenth century, London had begun spreading out into rural areas of Surrey and Kent. The nineteenth century saw a rapid extension of this process as the City proper, the "square mile" formerly confined by the city wall, was given over to shops, offices and warehouses. In the West End, fashionable squares and town houses were completed. The growing middle classes built houses in suburbs such as Camberwell, Paddington and Clapham. Although the East End, [7] including Whitechapel, Bethnal Green and Stepney, continued to grow, the working classes too began moving to districts on the edge of the built-up area, such as Hammersmith.

Railways and transport

The growth of suburban London was greatly accelerated by the coming of the railways [1], which soon spread out into a dense network. The first underground line in the world, from Paddington to Fenchurch Street, was opened by the Metropolitan Railway Company in 1863 and in the first six weeks carried an average of 26,000 passengers a day. A first-class fare between Edgware Road and King's Cross was sixpence. In 1864 special workmen's trains were introduced with a maximum return fare of only threepence. Other lines soon connected the main line stations and all important parts of the metropolis. The first electrified line opened in 1890. By the end of the century horse-drawn buses and trams provided alternative transport [Key].

The central area of the capital was refurnished with a series of new public buildings,

CONNECTIONS

See also
Social reform 1800-1914
Victoria and her statesmen

In other volumes
The Industrial Revolution (29)
Realist painting in the 19th century (35)
European architecture in the 19th century (35)

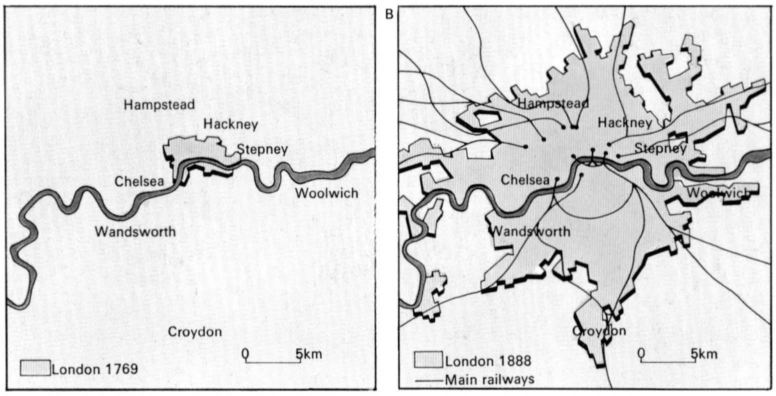

1A
Hampstead
Hackney
Stepney
Chelsea
Woolwich
Wandsworth
Croydon
0 5km
London 1769

B
Hampstead
Hackney
Stepney
Chelsea
Woolwich
Wandsworth
Croydon
0 5km
London 1888
Main railways

1 Railways grew out of urban expansion but also created it. The London and Greenwich line, opened in 1836, was London's first steam-powered railway. By 1852, most of today's mainline stations were in being and there were several suburban lines. From 1863 the Underground system provided rapid transport in the metropolitan area. In 1880, between 150 and 170 million rail journeys were made in the city annually.

2 Cholera epidemics in the 1830s and 1840s gave an important stimulus to the public health system. Royal Commissions of inquiry led to the creation of a General Board of Health and a Medical Officer of Health in 1848, in spite of opposition from the City of London. Improvements in water supply and sanitation followed. Until the 1860s, London's sewers were discharged into the Thames.

4 The Bank of England, established in 1694 to finance a war with France, was subsequently granted a monopoly of joint stock banking. While smaller banks were restricted to only six partners between 1708 and 1826, it became government banker and reserve bank for the whole country – a status ratified in the Bank Charter Act (1844). The fine buildings, completed in 1827, are imposing examples of the many public buildings erected in London during the 19th century. Others, in Victorian neo-Gothic style include St Pancras Station (1865–71) and the Royal Courts of Justice (1871–82).

3 A professional police force for London was created under the Metropolitan Police Act of 1829. Until then, London had only a few hundred professional police. The security of the capital largely depended upon an unco-ordinated band of watchmen and constables under several different authorities. The Act enabled a unified policing of the whole metropolitan area, with the exception of the City proper, using several thousand professional police officers

5 London fashion set the pattern of taste and consumption for the country as a whole. The mass market in the capital stimulated the rise of large department stores in the 1880s along bustling streets such as Regent Street, shown here. During the 19th century small, family-run shops began to disappear. They either developed as chain stores, such as J. Sainsbury's, which first opened in Drury Lane in 1869, or they were replaced by large, independent department stores.

including the rebuilt Houses of Parliament (1836–67), the Royal Courts (1871–82), the Bank of England (1795–1827) [4] and the great museums in Kensington. Trafalgar Square was completed in the 1840s. Widened streets, notably the Embankment [8], imitated the boulevards of Paris and some of the old slums were cleared to make way for new streets such as Charing Cross Road. Sewerage [8], lighting, paving and water supply were gradually brought under control after the cholera epidemics of the 1830s and 1840s [2]. The establishment of a Metropolitan Board of Works in 1855 was important for unified planning.

Social reforms

The vitality and commercial prosperity of the capital were reflected only slowly in social reforms. As people crowded into the terrace houses thrown up by speculative builders around gasworks, breweries or warehouses, the parishes of the East End became spawning grounds for crime and disease. General William Booth (1829–1912), who founded the Salvation Army in 1878 to reconvert the slum dwellers called them the people of "darkest England". In that year, while many landowners were earning £100,000 a year and paying tax of only 2d in the pound, the average labourer's income was £70. Fashionable strollers [5] wore hand-sewn garments created by sweated labour paid at a rate of only 2d an hour.

In 1885, it was estimated that one in four Londoners still lived in abject poverty. Only after 1880, when primary education became compulsory, were the streets cleared of ragged children living on their wits.

Despite the ferocious penalties for even petty crime, an estimated 100,000 in London lived by thieving or swindling in the 1860s, and another 80,000 were prostitutes. Sensational stories of crime and capture by the Metropolitan Police Force [3] could be read daily in the "penny dreadfuls". This was the fog-shrouded city of Sweeny Todd the Barber and Jack the Ripper. Violent riots by the unemployed in 1886 and 1887 gave belated vent to the distress that went hand-in-hand with the music halls [6], gin palaces and imperial pomp of Victorian London.

St Paul's Cathedral, erected in more spacious days, looks down on the Fleet Street of 1900 when vehicles thronged London's streets and traffic jams had become common. In 1850 there were more than 1,000 horse-drawn buses at work in the capital as well as countless carts and wagons. Congestion was one indication of the need for a new form of urban planning. London was the first industrial metropolis to have to cope with the problems of public health, urban transport, housing and other services on a mass scale. The unprecedented difficulties created by its growth necessitated a dramatic increase in the powers of local government.

6

7

6 Music halls became immensely popular in the 19th century. After a licensing Act in 1843, music halls, unlike theatres, could serve alcohol. The first commercial halls were the Canterbury in Lambeth (1852) and the Oxford Music Hall in Oxford Street (1861). Forty halls were taking in custom in London in 1868, and as the century progressed, music halls came to be more widely accepted as an alternative to the theatre.

7 The East End of London remained notorious for its poverty and bad housing well into this century. Many of its inhabitants were immigrants who had come from Ireland and continental Europe.

8

8 Construction of the Embankment along the River Thames (started 1867) with railways, sewerage and other services was a rare example of a united planning for growth. An efficient London system of drainage and sewerage was delayed by a lack of centralized authority. In 1858, work began on a complete system of sewerage for the capital. This great engineering feat was completed in 1865 and cost £4 million, with 131km of pipes carrying 1,703 million litres of sewage each day.

9

9 London was the social centre of Britain. The London "season" attracted wealthy families up from the country to reside in the substantial houses they kept in town. Hyde Park (shown here) was a fashionable place of recreation.

The fight for the vote

The early nineteenth-century parliamentary system in Britain contained many anomalies. The right to vote was governed by a complex system of traditional rights and privileges that had hardly changed since the mid-seventeenth century. Many boroughs elected their MPs on a tiny franchise; some had become so reduced that they were known as "rotten" boroughs and election to the seat lay almost entirely within the power of the local landowner. Moreover, the dramatic growth and redistribution in population during the Industrial Revolution created an anomalous situation where large, thriving towns had no representation whatsoever in Parliament.

Twin aspects of reform

Parliamentary reform, therefore, had two major aspects; the progressive extension of the franchise, to encompass all men, and later women; and the redistribution of seats to rectify the anomalies of the "unreformed" House of Commons. In addition, the conduct of elections, the use of bribery, and the decisive power of individual patrons in the many "pocket" boroughs all formed part of the long-standing unreformed system.

Movements for reform began in the second half of the 1700s, when the radical demagogue John Wilkes (1727–97) whipped up much popular support in London in the 1760s and 1770s. Fear of disorder, following the French Revolution, and the vested interests of many existing MPs, held back reform for another generation. But reform and "radical" ideas were kept alive by men such as Henry Hunt (1773–1835), William Cobbett (1763–1835), John Cartwright (1740–1824), and Francis Place (1771–1854).

The growth of the manufacturing towns during the Napoleonic Wars created a demand for representation, seen in the formation of political unions in towns such as Birmingham and Manchester. Discontent with the Tory administrations brought the Whigs to power in 1830.

A bill was introduced in 1831 but was rejected by the House of Lords. This caused widespread unrest, including riots at Derby, Nottingham and Bristol. Under threat of the creation of new peers, the Reform Bill was passed in 1832. The First Reform Act replaced the existing confusion of voting qualifications with a more regular system. But the electorate rose to only 652,000 and power remained vested in the hands of the upper and middle classes. More significant was the redistribution of 143 seats from the worst of the insignificant rotten boroughs to the larger manufacturing towns, London, and the counties [1, 2].

The 1832 Reform Act was in many ways conservative. Even many Whigs regarded it only as a measure to cure the anomalies of the existing electoral system. Attempts by the Chartists to coerce Parliament into a further programme of radical reform was resisted by the propertied classes. Three mass petitions in 1839, 1842 and 1848 [3] in support of the Charter were ignored.

The vote for the working man

Growing prosperity brought more people within the 1832 franchise qualifications by the 1860s. With the increasing inevitability of a further measure of reform, the Conserva-

CONNECTIONS

See also
Pitt, Fox and the call for reform
The British Labour Movement to 1868
Social reform 1800-1914
Victoria and her statesmen
The British Labour Movement 1868-1930

In other volumes
Political thought in the 19th century (29)
Evolution of the Western democracies (29)

1 The post-1832 "reformed" Parliament had members from the previously unrepresented manufacturing towns at the expense of the small "rotten" boroughs and some "pocket" boroughs.

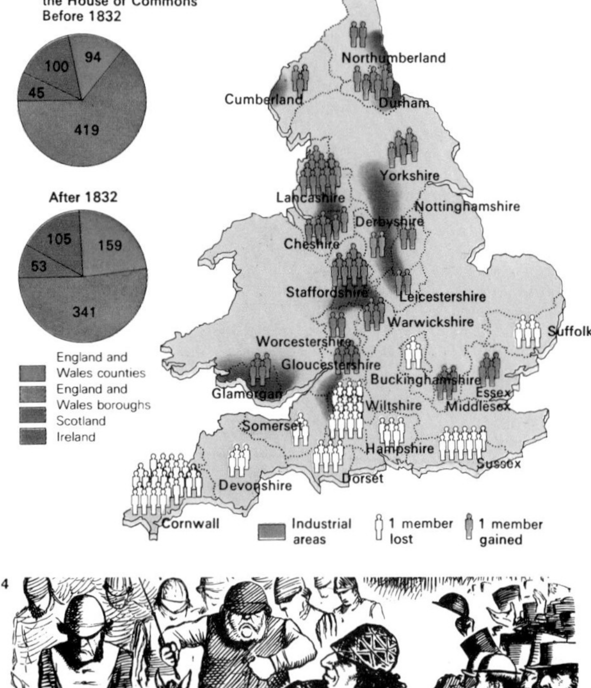

2 The First Reform Bill was essentially a conservative measure. It rectified the anomalies created by the population changes in the previous hundred years and enfranchised the upper middle classes.

3 The Chartists, here shown at their last great meeting in 1848, demanded sweeping electoral reforms; but the movement died because of dissension and poor leadership.

4 Disraeli leads "the race for electoral reform" in this Punch cartoon. The Second Reform Bill was passed in 1867 by the Conservatives under Derby and Disraeli.

tive leaders, Lord Derby (1799–1869) and Benjamin Disraeli (1804–81), and the Liberal leader, William Gladstone (1809–98), juggled with the new proposals to win advantage for their parties. It was Disraeli who finally managed to keep his party together and who is credited with the Second Reform Act in 1867 [4]. This act extended the vote to about one million urban working men, a further redistribution of seats.

The Ballot Act of 1872 introduced secret ballot, and in 1883 the worst aspects of electoral corruption were made illegal. In 1884 the Third Reform Act was passed by the Liberals, which enfranchised agricultural labourers and increased the electorate from about three million to about five million. In the following year, another redistribution of seats removed the last proprietary boroughs. Finally, in 1918 all men over the age of 21 received the vote [8].

The suffragette movement

Women had been excluded from the vote in all the reform acts up to 1918. They still had very insecure property rights and were widely regarded as unfit to exercise the responsibilities of political power [6]. The Women's Social and Political Union was founded in Manchester in 1903 to fight for the vote, headed by Mrs Emmeline Pankhurst (1858–1928) [7]. Known as "suffragettes", they gradually gave up normal methods of demonstrations and propaganda and turned to violence, breaking windows, setting building on fire, chaining themselves to railings, and resisting arrest.

With the defeat of a moderate proposal for female suffrage in 1912, the campaign for women's rights was temporarily frustrated. World War I, however, advanced the status of women. They played an immense part in the war effort, working in munitions factories and previously male-dominated jobs. In 1918 women over 30 were given the vote; and this franchise was extended to all women over 21 in 1928.

Plural voting, through property or businesses in more than one constituency, was abolished in 1906; it finally disappeared in 1948 with the removal of university seats at Oxford and Cambridge.

KEY

The introduction of secret voting (1872) was one of the several reforms that had removed the worst abuses from the electoral system by the end of the 1800s. But women – half the population – still did not have the vote. After 1884, more than half the adult males were eligible to vote: the redistribution of seats had corrected the worst imbalances produced by the growth of the industrial towns that occurred during the Industrial Revolution. One result of these and other reforms, such as the abolition of a property qualification for MPs (1858), was the rise of the Labour Party.

5 Ramsay Macdonald (1866–1937) [centre] formed the first Labour government in January 1924. The Labour Party achieved an electoral breakthrough in the 1906 general election, when they formed a pact with the Liberals. Labour's 30 seats at that election were a recognition of the growing power of a party that represented the interests of the newly enfranchised working classes.

6 The question of votes for women became a prominent issue in the ten years prior to 1914 when women's groups were formed to campaign for the "suffrage". This was not fully achieved, for women over 21, until 1928.

7 Mrs Emmeline Pankhurst, leader of the suffragettes, is carried away by the police during a demonstration. After 1905, the suffragettes pursued a militant policy, which led to a number of arrests and imprisonments.

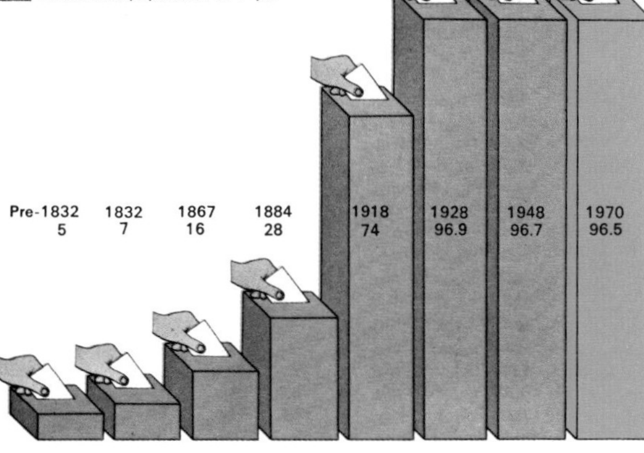

8 The electorate only gradually increased with the passing of the Reform Acts of 1832, 1867 and 1884. Growing economic prosperity brought many within the franchise qualifications without the need of legislation. In 1918, men over 21 and all women over 30 years old were granted the vote. In 1928 all women over 21 were given the vote. In 1948 the last remnant of plural voting was abolished and, as a result, the number of the electorate fell to some extent.

9 A contemporary election poster graphically portrays the conflict in 1909 between the Conservative-dominated House of Lords and the Liberal government; it reached a climax when the Lords rejected the government's budget. Two elections were forced, and on each occasion the Liberals were returned. In 1911 the primacy of the elected assembly was established when, under threat of the creation of more peers, a bill was passed restricting the powers of the Lords.

Ireland from Union to Partition

The legislatures of Dublin and London were combined on 1 January 1801 for reasons of state – British reasons, although the Union also suited those Protestants of the Irish Ascendancy who feared the rising forces of Catholicism and democracy. Other Irish Protestants opposed the measure, distrusting Westminster's will to preserve Protestant privileges, while Catholic leaders tended to favour Union, accompanied as it was to be by legislation to grant Catholics the right to sit in the Union Parliament.

Consequences of the Union

In the event, Protestant fears of the Union turned out to be as unfounded as Catholic hopes. Protestants continued to represent Irish constituencies in Parliament, the Anglican Church remained established and the separate Irish administration continued to favour Protestant interests.

To Catholics, the Union provided scant blessing. Their right to sit in Parliament was not conceded, the prime minister, the younger William Pitt (1759–1806) preferring to resign rather than jeopardize the war effort against France by provoking a constitutional crisis over King George III's (reigned 1760–1820) opposition to Catholic emancipation. Emancipation became, therefore, a principal issue of the Union Parliament: its denial completely disenchanted Catholics with the Union [1].

The land problem and Home Rule

The Great Famine of 1845–49 [2] stressed the enduring problem of nineteenth-century Ireland – the imbalance of its land and people. The Irish population had grown alarmingly from five-and-a-half million in 1800 to more than eight million by 1845. Crowded together in smallholdings subdivided into uneconomic units, increasingly dependent upon a potato diet, the Catholic labourers and tenant farmers presented a desperate spectacle. Without industrial alternatives, the peasantry had to remain on the land, exposed to periodic crop failures.

At Westminster, tenant and Catholic spokesmen tried to co-ordinate Irish MPs to deal with Irish issues, but, in practice, allegiance to the Liberal and Tory parties prevailed. But after the false start of Isaac Butt's (1813–79) Home Rule League (1873), Charles Stewart Parnell (1846–91) [5] welded together a disciplined Irish Party in pursuit of Home Rule.

As a result of the long-felt grievance over ownership, unsatisfactory tenancy arrangements, misguided legislation, a further series of bad harvests from 1877, and the organization of the Irish National Land League, rural discontent was brought to a new focus between 1879–82 [4]. Parnell yoked this to his parliamentary demands, while the shadowy Irish Republican Brotherhood (the Fenian movement) begun by James Stephens (1825–1901) in 1858 and now given direction by John Devoy (1842–1928) from America, lent clandestine support. Coercion proved an insufficient government response but the Liberal leader, William Gladstone (1809–98), accepting the logic of Parnell's position, attempted in vain to devolve a Home Rule parliament to Dublin [6].

Meanwhile, the Home Rule Party, split in 1890 and discredited by internal feuds, was being outflanked by other movements

CONNECTIONS

See also
The English in Ireland
Pitt, Fox and the call for reform
Victoria and her statesmen
Scotland in the 19th century

In other volumes
Irish culture since 1850

1

1 Daniel O'Connell (1775-1847), the first politician in the British Isles to mobilize mass support behind his cause, won Catholic emancipation in 1829. As MP for Clare, he alternately bargained for reforms and attacked the Union itself. But support for his Repeal Association declined after 1843 when he refused to risk bloodshed in opposition to Westminster and the Union.

2

Famine statistics

Population (millions): 1844 – 8.3; 1847 – 8.0; 1850 – 6.9

Mortality (thousands): 75; 165; 250 — Total; Diarrhoea & dysentery; Fever & starvation

2 The Great Famine of 1845–9 was a disaster on an unprecedented scale in Irish history. Total figures for deaths and disease disguise the famine's uneven impact, most severe in the West and least damaging in the North East. In 1845–6 government action relieved starvation, but renewed crop failure overwhelmed the shadowy administrative structure. The ensuing horror generated intense hatred against Britain.

3

to USA; to other places; = 25,000

1851–60; 1861–70; 1871–80; 1881–90; 1891–1900

3 Inhibitions against emigration were broken by the Famine and a steady flow of emigrants began to leave Ireland. By 1911, when the population stabilized at nearly four-and-a-half million, more Irish lived in North America, Britain and the Empire than in Ireland. Their departure made possible a better standard of living in Ireland, and added an international dimension to Irish nationalism.

4

4 Eviction of tenants was common in the 1870s and 1880s when conflicts between tenant farmers and landlords were at their sharpest. Landlords did not consolidate sufficiently, being effectively restrained by popular opposition, but with tenants of tiny holdings unable to live, let alone pay rent, amalgamation into viable farms was the only economic solution. The Land League seized on the evictions to focus mass resentment against the landlord system.

5

5 Charles Stewart Parnell, MP for Meath from 1875, led 59 Irish MPs at Westminster by 1880, soon moulding them into a disciplined, salaried party (86 strong at its height), pledged to support Home Rule. Backed by constituency branches, mass Land League support and secret Fenian co-operation, he made Home Rule credible, and in 1886 won the Liberal Party over to this cause. Parnell lost Catholic support after he was cited in a divorce case in 1890.

working to "de-Anglicize" Ireland and to win complete independence. In 1906 Arthur Griffith (1872–1922) succeeded in mobilizing disparate political groupings into his own movement, Sinn Fein, dedicated to economic self-sufficiency and political withdrawal from the Union.

Yet, even while Sinn Fein gathered strength, the Home Rule Party, shamed into unity in 1900 under the leadership of John Redmond (1856–1918), received renewed authority from political circumstances in Britain. The return of the Liberals there in 1906 made Home Rule again a possibility.

Ireland divided

From 1912 onwards, tension grew first with the Protestant Unionists arming [7], then Home Rulers – the one to prevent, the other to enforce a bill expected to become law in 1914. Only the outbreak of World War I subsumed this minor quarrel within a mightier conflict. The operation of Home Rule was postponed until the end of the war.

Before that, however, republicans, socialists and other separatists had risen in 1916 [8] to proclaim an independent Irish Republic. They were quickly crushed and their leaders executed, but these groups re-formed in 1917 to merge under the Sinn Fein banner.

The Home Rule Party, compromised by its attachment to the British war effort and the indecisive leadership of the dying Redmond, could not be saved from humiliation in the post-war elections. But Sinn Fein, while winning 73 seats to the Party's 6, could not prevent the Unionists from winning 26 in the North East.

Prime minister Lloyd George (1863–1945) belatedly turned again to Ireland in 1919. In 1920 he created two Home Rule parliaments: one in Dublin for 26 of Ireland's 32 counties; the other in Belfast for the remainder in the North East. Reluctantly, Northern Unionists accepted this compromise, although they had been committed to preserving the 9-county Province of Ulster from Dublin rule. Contemptuously, Southern Nationalists, by now sworn to win a 32-county Irish Republic, refused either to accept the limited powers offered or the partition of the island involved.

KEY

POBLACHT NA H EIREANN.

THE PROVISIONAL GOVERNMENT OF THE IRISH REPUBLIC TO THE PEOPLE OF IRELAND.

IRISHMEN AND IRISHWOMEN: In the name of God and of the dead generations from which she receives her old tradition of nationhood, Ireland, through us, summons her children to her flag and strikes for her freedom.

Having organised and trained her manhood through her secret revolutionary organisation, the Irish Republican Brotherhood, and through her open military organisations, the Irish Volunteers and the Irish Citizen Army, having patiently perfected her discipline, having resolutely waited for the right moment to reveal itself, she now seizes that moment, and, supported by her exiled children in America and by gallant allies in Europe, but relying in the first on her own strength, she strikes in full confidence of victory.

We declare the right of the people of Ireland to the ownership of Ireland, and to the unfettered control of Irish destinies, to be sovereign and indefeasible. The long usurpation of that right by a foreign people and government has not extinguished the right, nor can it ever be extinguished except by the destruction of the Irish people. In every generation the Irish people have asserted their right to national freedom and sovereignty; six times during the past three hundred years they have asserted it in arms. Standing on that fundamental right and again asserting it in arms in the face of the world, we hereby proclaim the Irish Republic as a Sovereign Independent State, and we pledge our lives and the lives of our comrades-in-arms to the cause of its freedom, of its welfare, and of its exaltation among the nations.

The Irish Republic is entitled to, and hereby claims, the allegiance of every Irishman and Irishwoman. The Republic guarantees religious and civil liberty, equal rights and equal opportunities to all its citizens, and declares its resolve to pursue the happiness and prosperity of the whole nation and of all its parts, cherishing all the children of the nation equally, and oblivious of the differences carefully fostered by an alien government, which have divided a minority from the majority in the past.

Until our arms have brought the opportune moment for the establishment of a permanent National Government, representative of the whole people of Ireland and elected by the suffrages of all her men and women, the Provisional Government, hereby constituted, will administer the civil and military affairs of the Republic in trust for the people.

We place the cause of the Irish Republic under the protection of the Most High God, Whose blessing we invoke upon our arms, and we pray that no one who serves that cause will dishonour it by cowardice, inhumanity, or rapine. In this supreme hour the Irish nation must, by its valour and discipline and by the readiness of its children to sacrifice themselves for the common good, prove itself worthy of the august destiny to which it is called.

Signed on Behalf of the Provisional Government,
THOMAS J. CLARKE.
SEAN Mac DIARMADA. THOMAS MacDONAGH.
P. H. PEARSE. EAMONN CEANNT.
JAMES CONNOLLY. JOSEPH PLUNKETT.

On Easter Monday 24 April 1916, Irish republicans, socialists and other separatists rose in armed revolt against British rule in Ireland. The rebellion was quickly crushed, the last rebel strongholds surrendering to British troops six days after the republic had been proclaimed (the proclamation is shown here). In the fighting, 100 British troops and 450 Irish were killed. The rebel leaders were executed, notably Patrick Pearse (1879–1916) and James Connolly (1870–1916). Only Eamon de Valera (1882–1975) survived because he had been born in the USA. However these measures, in the aftermath of the rebellion, won Irish opinion to the republican cause.

6

6 William Gladstone, seen in the cartoon struggling with the Irish question, became absorbed with Irish affairs after 1886 and his unsuccessful first Home Rule Bill. Prior to that, in 1869, he had disestablished the Irish Church and passed Land Acts, in 1870 and 1881, which gave tenants greater security and legally fixed rents. In 1893 he introduced the second Home Rule Bill, which was rejected by the House of Lords.

7

7 Edward Carson (1854–1935) led the Ulster Unionists from 1910–20, pledging and arming them to resist Home Rule in any form. In 1914 his offer to accept Home Rule with the exclusion of Ulster was rejected. In 1916 he reduced this demand to only the six most Protestant Ulster counties. Although Carson preferred continued integration with the United Kingdom, he accepted the creation of a separate parliament for the six counties in Belfast in 1920.

8

8 The Easter Rising of 24–29 April 1916, led by the Irish Volunteers and the Irish Citizen Army, seized several public buildings in the centre of Dublin before surrendering to the British army. Although many Irish people were out of sympathy with the insurrection itself, support for the republican cause grew after the secret execution of the seven signatories of the Proclamation of the Irish Republic and eight other rebel leaders, and widespread arrests.

9

9 Michael Collins (1890–1922) (right) was a leader of the Irish struggle for independence. After 1916 he became involved in Sinn Fein politics and was elected to the Dail in 1919, becoming a leading member of the provisional government. Eamon de Valera (left) was the senior surviving officer of the 1916 rising and principal Irish leader. He became President of Sinn Fein in 1917, and President of the Republic and of Dáil Eireann (Irish lower house) in 1919.

Scotland in the 19th century

The political framework of nineteenth-century Scotland continued to be union with England but, by the end of the century, in place of the handful of privileged voters who had elected MPs under the old regime, something approaching a democracy based on adult male suffrage had been achieved. This had been the work of successive Reform Bills in 1832, 1867 and 1884. Eventually Scotland was electing 72 MPs from constituencies that gave weight to the Scottish urban population, and its share of the Westminster parliament – 670 MPs – fairly reflected the Scottish proportion of British population.

The beginnings of socialism

Following the triumph of the Whigs under Francis Jeffrey (1773–1850) and Henry Cockburn (1779–1854) at the time of the Great Reform Bill of 1832, Scotland settled down to become loyally Liberal – 53 MPs were elected under William Ewart Gladstone's colours compared to seven Conservatives in 1880, although the split in the party over Irish Home Rule in 1886 shook this allegiance seriously. At the same time there was a Scottish radical tradition to the left of this mainstream.

It surfaced at the time of the so-called Radical War in 1820, which was really a combination of a strike and a small abortive rising in the Glasgow area. It was seen again with the Chartists between 1838 and 1848, although the Scottish Chartists mainly disapproved of physical force and sought reformation through temperance and democracy. And in 1888 socialism struck root with the foundation of the Scottish Labour Party and the rise of Keir Hardie (1856–1915) [9] who later became the leader of the British Independent Labour Party (ILP) in 1893. Trade unionism grew rapidly, especially in skilled trades and among the cotton spinners and miners, although a Scottish Trades Union Congress (with 40,000 members) was not founded until 1897.

Generally speaking, there was little dissatisfaction over union with Britain, although because Westminster was increasingly obliged to legislate for Scottish affairs as the problems of industrial society became more complex (by reforming the Poor Law in 1845 and the school system in 1872, for example) there was more demand for specifically Scottish experts in the government. This was met in 1885 by the creation of a Secretary of State for Scotland and a Scottish Office based in London and Edinburgh. A small nationalist movement arose at the end of the century; few took it seriously, although Hardie and other early socialists also favoured Home Rule. For many Scots, Church politics were more significant than national ones; the Disruption of the Church of Scotland in 1843 [5] into the Established Church and the Free Church over the question of who should choose the ministers generated enormous excitement.

The prosperity of heavy industries

The Scottish economy in the nineteenth century was highly successful: to the original base of cotton textiles an important iron industry in the West Central Belt was added in the 1830s, and after 1870 the vitality of the shipyards and steelworks of Clydeside and of jute round Dundee prevented the country from slipping into recession [3]. A third of all

CONNECTIONS

See also
Scotland in the 18th century
The fight for the vote
The British Labour Movement 1868-1930

In other volumes
The Industrial Revolution (29)
Scottish culture to 1850 (34)
Scottish culture since 1850 (35)

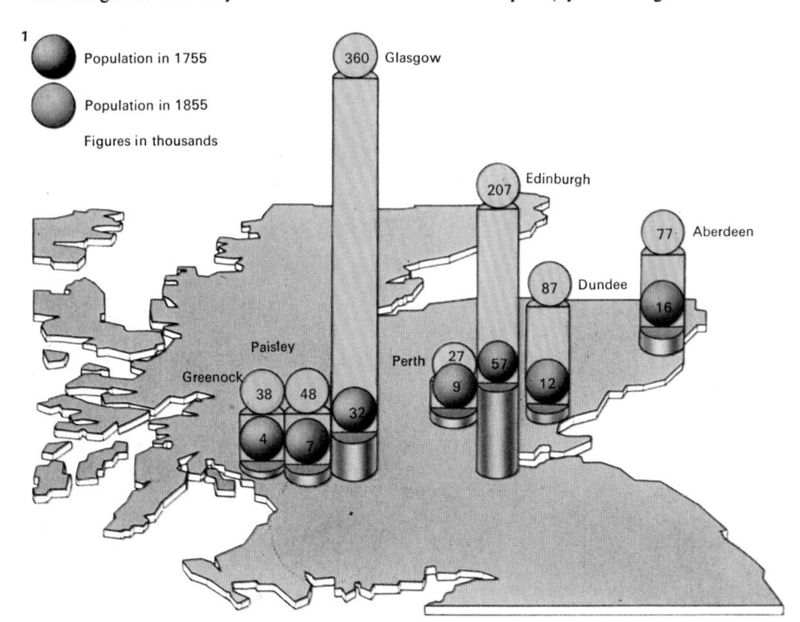

1 Industrialization in Scotland was accompanied by rapid urbanization, not so much in the foundation of new towns as in the very rapid growth of old ones: Glasgow, for example, had 23,000 inhabitants by about 1750, when it was already the second town of Scotland, but it had 329,000 by 1851. Nevertheless there were new towns, which often grew very fast. Airdrie, for instance, had a population of 1,200 in 1755, but with the development of iron and coal in Lanarkshire, it exceeded 13,000 by 1851. But primitive sanitation, unimproved from a previous era, menaced the growing towns and ominously increased mortality.

2 The Highlands' economy collapsed in the early 1800s and this resulted in a grim outlook for crofters such as these. Prices for three of their four main staples – cattle, kelp and fish – had fallen disastrously, and only wool was still viable. This meant that wealthy sheep farmers from the Lowlands began to introduce their animals into the crofters' fertile plots. As a result, the green summer pastures were quickly overcropped. The crofters themselves were usually evicted to the outskirts. Such evictions were sometimes executed considerately, but at other times the action was ruthless, causing great hardship.

3

Coal (million tonnes)
Iron (million tonnes)

1850
7.4
0.5

1870
14.9
1.2

1890
24.3
0.7

3 Economic growth in early Victorian Scotland was firmly based on Scottish natural resources, but with the invention of cheap steel after 1870 many of the ores had to be imported from various countries. The soaring indices of production point to an economy increasingly dependent on a narrow base of heavy industry. For example, by 1900 much of the metal went into the great ships being built in the yards along the Clyde.

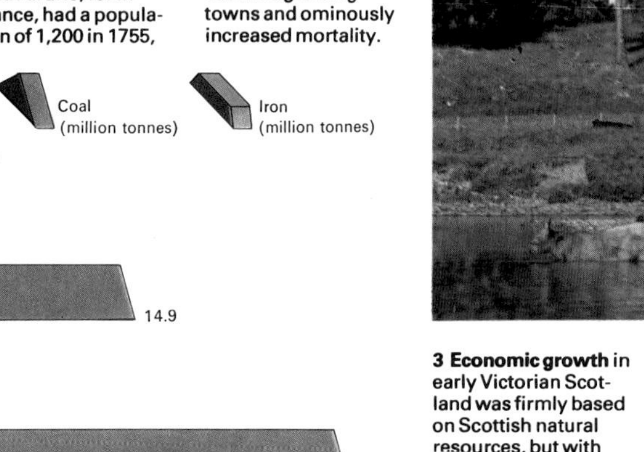

4 Balmoral Castle, built in Scottish Baronial style about 80km west of Aberdeen on the River Dee, appealed greatly to Queen Victoria's love of the romantic. In 1856 she wrote of it in her diary: "Every year my heart becomes more fixed in this dear paradise...and so much so now, that *all* has become my dear Albert's *own* creation...". The castle replaced a smaller one bought by Albert for the royal family in 1852.

ships built in Britain were being built on the Clyde by 1913. The Scots had earned much lower incomes than the English in 1800, but by 1900 the average working man on the Clyde was probably at least as well paid as the average English worker. This sense of prosperity made Glasgow an enormously self-confident business capital – few Scottish firms were controlled from elsewhere – but concealed the fact that Scottish wealth rested on a narrow base of heavy industries.

The improverished Highlands

The reverse side of the coin was the patchy nature of the wealth. Throughout the Highlands people were very poor: the population increased until 1841, far outstripping the growth of resources, and then collapsed after the potato famine of 1846. Thousands of small-scale tenants were evicted in the "clearances" to make way for sheep [2]; tens of thousands emigrated [6]. By the 1870s and 1880s over-intensive sheep farming had run down the fertility of the land and this, coupled with a dramatic slump in grain and wool prices, led to even further depopulation of the Highlands regions through migration.

Meanwhile those who left were partly balanced by those who arrived. These were Irishmen immigrating into the coalfields and factories of central Scotland where they generally had to take the lowest paid labouring jobs. The urban poor had a hard time; the slums of the great cities were probably the worst in Europe even when the economy was booming [Key, 1].

To the outside world, however, there were perhaps two main symbols of nineteenth century Scotland: Balmoral [4], where Queen Victoria gloried in a romantic view of the Highlands far removed from the unpleasant realities of the black houses of the Isle of Lewis; and Scottish science and medicine at the universities. Men such as Lord Kelvin (1824–1907) at Glasgow, or James Clerk Maxwell (1831–79), the physicist who was professor at Aberdeen, King's College, London and Cambridge, vied in their reputations with Joseph Lister (1827-1912) [7] and James Simpson (1811-70), the first to use chloroform in obstetrics and the first in Britain to use ether.

KEY

The industries and slums of Clydeside were the central paradox of 19th-century Scotland. On the one hand they produced the greatest wealth Scotland had ever known – by 1906 wage rates were higher than in most of England. On the other hand, they had a population whose housing conditions were worse than any in Britain: even in 1911 two-thirds of the population lived in houses that had only one or two rooms.

5

5 Thomas Chalmers (1789–1847) was a widely influential theologian and preacher. He was for years head of the evangelical wing of the Church of Scotland, and then founded the Free Church which broke off at the Disruption of 1843. He abandoned the established church because of its traditional method of choosing ministers – he preferred democratic elections. Within Britain he was celebrated for his book, *Christian and Civic Economy of Large Towns*, which encouraged the middle classes to believe that the problems of poverty could be cured by generous philanthropic action with a rigorous inquiry into the personal and moral condition of the individual poor.

6

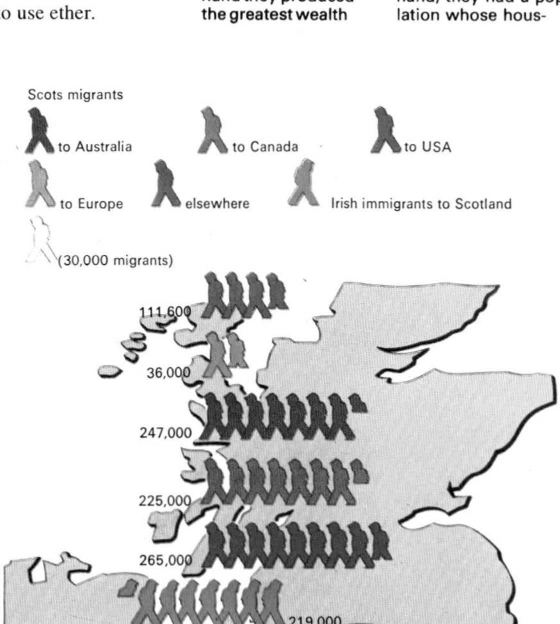

6 Nineteenth-century Scotland was like a bath with the taps full on and the plug out. There was a rapid natural increase accompanied by an inrush of Irish immigrants to the looms, mines and ironworks of the Central Belt. At the same time, many native Scots, especially Gaelic-speaking Highlanders unwilling to move to an unfamiliar urban life, chose to go to Canada, and also to Australia, the USA and New Zealand. This outflowing tide resulted not so much from lack of opportunity at home as from the enticement of kinfolk already abroad. Few European nations apart from Ireland and Norway lost so much of their natural increase.

7

7 Joseph Lister (1827–1912) founded modern antiseptic surgery. When he went to work at Glasgow Infirmary in 1861 he found that nearly half the amputation cases died of post-operative gangrene. Lister eventually began to realize that pus formed as a result of infection by germs. He ensured that hands, instruments and dressings were sterilized. This, together with his introduction of sterilized catgut and carbolic acid as an antiseptic, after 1865, dramatically reduced surgical mortalities.

8

8 The decision of a handful of crofters to resist eviction by force in 1882 alarmed the government, who sent a gunboat to Skye to put down the "rising". It was cheered by the peasants, who believed that Queen Victoria had come to hear their grievances.

9

9 Keir Hardie (shown here) and R. B. Cunninghame Graham (1852–1936) were the fathers of socialism in Scotland. Hardie became leader of the British ILP and was described as "the best-hated and the best-loved man in Great Britain". In 1928 Cunninghame Graham helped to found the Scottish National Party. Hardie was a confirmed pacifist and was fervently opposed to the Boer War. He also favoured women's suffrage, and founded *The Labour Leader*, a Scottish newspaper.

Wales 1536-1914

The Acts of Union (1536–43) decreed that Wales henceforth was to be governed "in like form" to England. Wales was given a definite administrative boundary and was also unified politically within itself [Key]. The most progressive of the Welsh gentry were happy to be subsumed in a common British citizenship and voiced their gratitude to the Tudors for bringing order, stability and prosperity to Wales.

The power of the gentry

The gentry were the most powerful element within society and the task of administering local government remained in their hands for some 350 years. Traditionally conservative, they supported the Crown through every event. During the English Civil Wars (1642–6, 1648) they fought for the king in order to protect their prosperity and security and, after the Restoration in 1660, they re-established a monopoly of influence on the society, economy and politics of Wales. Until the mid-nineteenth century political power lay in the hands of a narrow circle of landowning families, and the mass of society remained deferential to their will. Three developments – the growth of Nonconformism, the Industrial Revolution and the spread of political radicalism – undermined the foundation of this society.

From the sixteenth century onwards successive waves of Protestantism lapped over Wales. Much was achieved: Welsh became the language of religion, and the translation of the scriptures into the vernacular [1] fostered the growth of a Bible-reading public. With the coming of Methodism in the 1730s, Reformation ideas were propagated far more intensively [3]. In 1811, the Methodist movement was forced to sever its connection with the Anglican Church and, in the company of fellow Dissenters, spread widely into rural and industrial areas. Noncomformity became a popular movement so that by 1851 about 80 per cent of practising Christians in Wales were Nonconformists.

The Industrial Revolution in Wales

The second major factor that created modern Wales was the Industrial Revolution. Until the end of the eighteenth century Wales displayed the main features of a pastoral, pre-industrial economy: a primitive technology, a slow rate of technical development and a lack of capital. But the arrival of the Industrial Revolution after 1760 transformed the social and economic life of Wales. Financed largely by English entrepreneurs, industrial development focused on the chain of ironworks on the periphery of the South Wales coalfields and in north-east Wales, on the copper mines of Anglesey and the slate quarries of Caernarvonshire. The spread of canals and railways improved communications and hastened large-scale industrial expansion.

At the same time, population growth began to accelerate dramatically. It rose from 370,000 in 1670 to 586,000 in 1801. Small villages grew into booming towns: in 1801, Merthyr Tydfil, with a population of 7,705, was the largest town in Wales [4]. By 1861, 60 per cent of the Welsh people lived in industrial areas. The decline of the iron industry after 1850 was followed by the growth of new steelmaking processes and the massive expansion of the coal industry.

CONNECTIONS

See also
The British Labour Movement to 1868
Social reform 1800-1914
The fight for the vote

In other volumes
Wales to the Act of Union (26)
The arts in Wales (35)

1

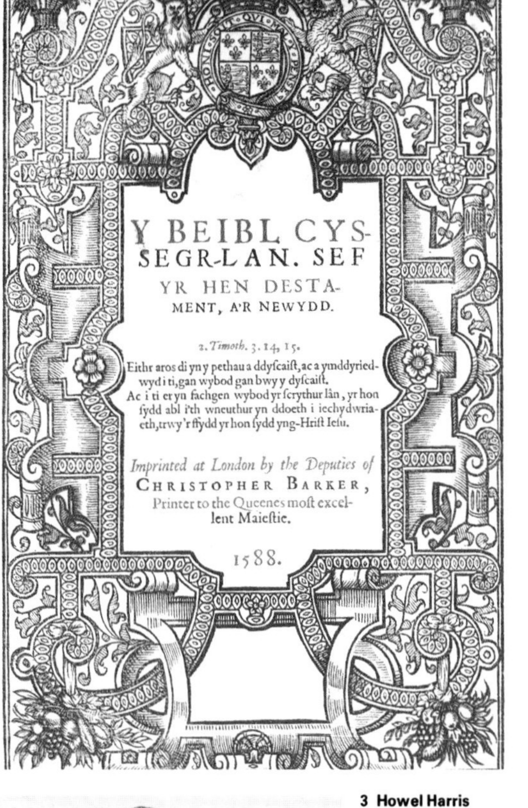

Y BEIBL CYS-SEGR-LAN. SEF YR HEN DESTA-MENT, A'R NEWYDD.

2. Timoth. 3. 14, 15.

Eithr aros di yn y pethau a ddyſcaiſt, ac a ymddyriedwyd i ti, gan wybod gan bwy y dyſcaiſt. Ac i ti er yn ſachgen wybod yr ſcrythur lân, yr hon ſydd abl i'th wneuthur yn ddoeth i iechydwriaeth, trwy'r ffydd yr hon ſydd yng-Hriſt Ieſu.

Imprinted at London by the Deputies of Christopher Barker, Printer to the Queenes moſt excellent Maieſtie.

1588.

2

1 The first Welsh Bible (1588) resulted from a statute in 1563 which ordered that the translation of the Bible into Welsh should be undertaken forthwith. The work was duly completed by an erudite Denbighshire vicar, William Morgan (*c.* 1545-1604). The translation provided a literary standard for future generations and ensured that Protestantism would be propagated in the Welsh language.

2 The Sker House, a large, bleak edifice close to the Kenfig Burrows in Glamorgan, is a good example of the many new or remodelled buildings which were constructed by the Welsh gentry in the 16th century. The house was built on a former monastic grange by the Turberville family. The economic and political power of the gentry at that time was reflected in their imposing country homes.

3

3 Howel Harris (1714–73) was the moving spirit behind the growth of Welsh Methodism. A fiery evangelist, Harris provided the movement with inspired leadership and an efficient organization.

4

4 The massive Cyfarthfa ironworks, founded in the mid-18th century, became the focal point of the iron-smelting town of Merthyr. In keeping with much of the Industrial Revolution in Wales, the works were financed by English capital.

As the unparalleled resources of the Rhondda valleys were plundered, coal came to dominate the Welsh economy. By 1912, coal output in the mining valleys of South Wales was more than 50 million tonnes.

Nationalism and political radicalism

The third factor was the growth of political radicalism, inspired by the revolutionary ideals formulated in France. Many processes hastened these ambitions: the Welsh press created an articulate and informed body of public opinion; acute economic distress in rural and industrial communities encouraged class awareness and a growing interest in political reform; and a slanderous government report – *The Treason of the Blue Books* in 1847 – injected new life into radicalism and awakened a sense of nationhood. The extension of the franchise in the nineteenth century gave radical Nonconformists the opportunity to undermine the landowning monopoly, to remove religious disabilities, and to create cultural and educational institutions attuned to Welsh circumstances and aspirations. Between 1868 and 1918 Welsh Liberals voiced the ambitions of a new Nonconformist middle and working class, and the response which they evoked from the electorate enabled them to erode the power of the old Anglican squirearchy and to capture the overwhelming majority of parliamentary seats in Wales.

As political nationalism spread in from Europe and Ireland, a new effort was made to emphasize the distinctiveness of Wales and to press for national equality and justice [7]. In Parliament, a ginger-group of young Liberals, led by Thomas Ellis (1859–89) and David Lloyd George (1863–1945) [8], called for religious equality, educational opportunity and land reform. Eventually, many gains were achieved: the Church in Wales was disestablished in 1920; Welsh universities, a National Library at Aberystwyth and a National Museum at Cardiff were established; a Welsh department was created within the Board of Education; and the concept of Wales was firmly established. By 1914 it was no longer considered to be a mere geographical term with neither institutions nor pride in its own nationhood.

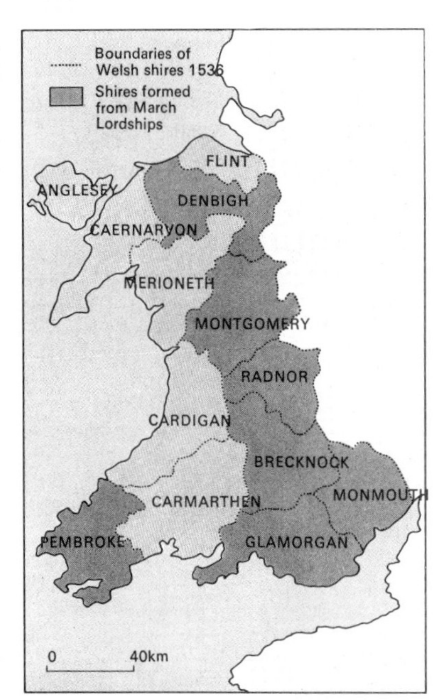

The Acts of Union incorporated Wales into England in order to achieve a more effective governance of Wales and the border area (Marches). Welshmen henceforth were to enjoy the rights and privileges of Englishmen; land was to be inherited according to the practice of primogeniture; and the whole of Wales was divided into shires — a framework that persisted until April 1974. English became the official language of law and government and English common law and methods of local administration were introduced. In return the new Welsh shires and boroughs could send 24 MPs to represent them in the English Parliament.

5 The Merthyr riot of 1831 developed from three main causes. First, discontent with the system of compelling workers to spend part of their wages in the expensive, company-owned shops; secondly, unemployment and the harsh provisions of the Poor Law; and thirdly unrest at the delay in passing the 1832 Reform Bill.

6 The Rebecca riots in the early 1840s occurred in separate places across south-west Wales. Disguised as women, small farmers protested against abuses of the turnpike system. They attacked the hated toll gates, burnt haystacks and threatened local magistrates. A government inquiry in 1844 resolved many of their grievances.

7 Michael D. Jones (1822–98) was one of the principal Welsh nationalists of the 19th century. He strove valiantly to persuade Welshmen to embrace a new, radical philosophy, to agitate for their political rights and to recover their self-respect and confidence. His determination to preserve national identity prompted him to establish a Welsh colony in Patagonia, South America, in 1865; this colony still exists as an isolated Welsh-speaking outpost today.

8 David Lloyd George, MP for Caernarvon boroughs from 1890, made his mark in politics as an enthusiastic champion of the rights of Welshmen, an enemy of privilege and as a "man of the people". As Chancellor of the Exchequer (1908-15) he introduced crucial social reforms, and his 1909 budget provoked an important constitutional crisis with the Lords. In 1916, he became the first Welshman to be appointed prime minister, which he remained until 1922. He earned a reputation as a courageous and decisive war leader, and a constructive peace-maker after World War I. His fertile mind and oratorial genius aroused widespread devotion and, equally, widespread dislike.

British foreign policy 1815-1914

The years between the final British victory over the French at Waterloo in 1815 and the outbreak of European war in 1914 are known by the British as the *Pax Britannica.* They were not years in which Britain was entirely free from war, but, defended around the globe by the world's most powerful navy, it faced no direct threat to its security. During this period, Britain's foreign secretaries played upon a world stage, able to take an enlarged view of their duties and so to weave into their strategic considerations matters of very wide political import.

Protecting free trade and the empire

For most of the century Britain was able to conduct its foreign affairs with mere deference to the views of other powers. Britain's main strategic aims were to protect the empire, in particular the trade route to India, and to maintain the balance of power in Europe. Liberal statesmen tried to encourage the progress of liberal nationalist movements in various parts of the world. But in general, foreign secretaries did not interfere in foreign disputes.

Britain was, of course, favourably placed by the conquests of the eighteenth century and the strength of the navy [5] to look upon the world as its oyster. The idea of free trade came to dominate not only the Exchequer, but also the Foreign Office. British statesmen considered the world as a place in which all nations, freely trading with one another, would learn that commercial interdependence had made war obsolete as an instrument of national policy.

Only as a result of mounting fear of Russian influence in the Mediterranean did Britain intervene in the war of Greek independence [1] in the 1820s and the Turko-Russian quarrel that led to the Crimean War (1854–6) [2, 3]. The nascent power of Russia and the debility of Turkey, the "sick man of Europe", were eventually to turn the Balkans into a powder keg. For a century the "Eastern question" smouldered.

British liberalism abroad

The tendencies of the age were revealed in the 1820s, during the foreign secretaryships of Viscount Castlereagh (1769–1822) and George Canning (1770–1827). Their main achievement was to disengage Britain from the conservative Holy Alliance of the despotic northern powers – Prussia, Austria and Russia. At the Congress of Verona (1822) Britain refused to support intervention in Spain to put down the liberal constitutional government that had toppled the Spanish Bourbons. Nor would it aid the "reactionary" cause in Sicily and Portugal. In Latin America Canning gave his blessing and recognition to the revolts against Spanish and Portuguese rule that ended in the establishment of the independent nations throughout the continent. Canning also lent his support to the Greek patriots who fought to gain their independence from the Ottoman Turks. He died two months before a combined British-French-Russian fleet destroyed a Turkish-Egyptian fleet in the harbour of Navarino (now Pilos, Greece) in 1827; Greece became an independent nation in 1832.

In 1830, Palmerston [Key] began his first term at the Foreign Office, which lasted until 1841. During it, his most notable achievement was to help Belgium win independence

CONNECTIONS

See also
Victoria and her statesmen

In other volumes
European empires in the 19th century (29)
German and Italian unification (29)
Europe 1870-1914 (29)
Balkanization and Slav nationalism (29)
Imperialism in the 19th century (30)
The British Empire in the 19th century (31)
Causes of World War I (31)

1 The revolt of the Greeks, epitomized in this painting by Delacroix, was the first liberal cause of the century that took England away from the alliance that had defeated Napoleon. Whereas Austria and Russia opposed Greek freedom, Castlereagh and Canning supported the revolt, and English sympathizers went to fight for the Greeks against the Turks – among them the poet Byron (1788–1824), who died there.

2 A Quaker deputation led by Joseph Sturge on the eve of the Crimean War (1854) paid a special visit to Tsar Nicholas I to plead for peace. This was unofficial, and although the British cabinet was divided on the issue, public opinion clamoured for war. Radical MPs who denounced it, including John Bright (1811–89) and Richard Cobden (1804–65), lost their seats at the election of 1857, in which Palmerston was safely returned.

3 The Crimean War revealed the inefficiency of the army's organization and command. More soldiers died from disease than in battle. This photograph shows Lt. Gen. Sir George Brown and his staff.

4 Giuseppe Garibaldi (1807–82), the Italian nationalist leader, visited London in 1864 and received a great popular welcome, addressing crowds of 20,000 at the Crystal Palace. Several other Continental revolutionaries and nationalists had a similar reception, including the Hungarian Louis Kossuth (1802–94), who fled to England after the Russians had invaded Hungary following Kossuth's proclamation of Hungarian independence from the Hapsburgs early in 1849. Despite his dubious political ambitions, Kossuth was entertained by the foreign secretary, Palmerston. Support for Continental nationalist movements was a potent force in domestic politics in the 19th century; sympathy for the Italians' struggle against the Austrians took Gladstone, who had previously been a Conservative, into the Liberal Party in 1859. Garibaldi's visit to London in 1864 quickened the demand for parliamentary reform; this was met in 1867.

from the Netherlands. (British guarantees to Belgium had fateful consequences in 1914). In the East, Palmerston sought to uphold the territorial rights of Turkey. For a time peace was maintained, but in 1854 Russia and Turkey went to war and Britain and France entered on the side of Turkey.

The Crimean War and after

The Crimean War was ostensibly about the tsar's claim to protect Christians under Turkish rule in Europe; in fact it was about whether Turkey should maintain its empire in Europe as a bulwark against Russian aggrandizement in the Balkans. The British army suffered terrible losses, but, in the end, Constantinople and the Black Sea were preserved from Russian control.

Twenty years later, when Turkish misrule in Bulgaria threatened war once more, Benjamin Disraeli (1804–81) went to the Congress of Berlin (1878) and brought back "peace with honour". The *status quo* was upheld without war, but Turkey's failure to learn the lesson and put its house in order and the rising appeal of Slav nationalism throughout the Balkans was a bleak omen.

By the 1880s British security was being undermined. The scramble by European powers for colonies in Africa had begun and in 1882 Britain occupied Egypt. Germany was cutting into Britain's trading and manufacturing supremacy, and was politically worrying France. At the end of Victoria's reign, Germany started building up its naval strength.

As the German threat grew, fears of Russia receded. The Foreign Office was led to recast its priorities, and "splendid isolation" became a thing of the past. In 1904 Edward VII's diplomacy was instrumental in securing the Entente Cordiale with France. There were many people, among them Joseph Chamberlain (1836–1914), who hankered after a German partnership, but the current was flowing in the opposite direction. France was the ally of Russia and in 1907 Britain joined them in the Triple Entente. In 1908, when Bosnia-Hercegovina was annexed by Germany's ally, Austria-Hungary, against the wishes of Russia, the ground was prepared for World War I.

KEY

Viscount Palmerston (1784–1865) presided over British foreign policy longer than any other man in modern history. As foreign secretary (1830–41, 1846–51) and prime minister (1855–8, 1859–65), his policy rested on confidence in the global pre-eminence of mid-Victorian Britain. His forthright defence of British interests was expressed in the Don Pacifico debate (1850), when he used warships to protect a British citizen against the Greek government, and defended himself with the phrase *"Civis Brittanicus sum"* (I am a citizen of Britain), echoing the *"Civis Romanus sum"* of Imperial Rome. From that day until his death Palmerston was a national hero.

5

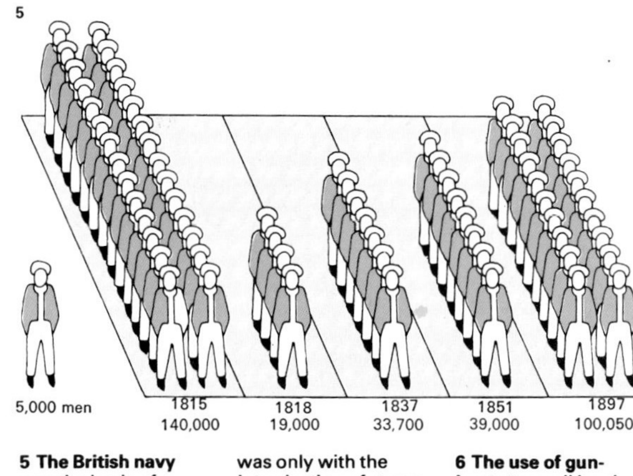

5 The British navy was the basis of the nation's power throughout the century. But the overwhelming victory at Trafalgar meant that the navy did not need to be large to maintain its ascendancy. It was only with the introduction of steam-driven battleships in the 1880s, and the start of the naval building race with Germany that the navy again employed as many men as in the time of Nelson.

6

6 The use of gunboats to quell local disturbances throughout the world, as in this expedition up the Nile to relieve Khartoum in 1884, was typical of the *Pax Britannica* as maintained by Palmerston.

7

THE COLOSSUS OF WORDS.

7 William Ewart Gladstone (1809–98) is depicted here as the "Colossus of Words", whose policies of peace and liberalism serve as an inspiration for reform at home. His stirring opposition to the Bulgarian atrocities of 1876, when the Turks violently put down a nationalist revolt, was typical of the high moral tone of his political feelings, and led to his overthrow of the Conservative government four years later.

8

8 Edward VII's visit to Paris in 1903, and his meeting with the French foreign secretary, won him great affection from the French. It also paved the way to the signing of the Entente Cordiale in 1904, so ending the enmity between the nations.

9

9 Naval strength was an important issue in the election of 1910, as this poster shows. HMS *Dreadnought* first of a powerful new class of battleship, was completed in 1906.

World War I: Britain's role

Britain's small but professional expeditionary force of 100,000 men, commanded by Sir John French (1852–1925), landed in France on 14 August 1914, ten days after the declaration of war. With an insight that ran contrary to popular opinion, the War Minister, Lord Kitchener (1850–1916), was already telling the Cabinet that they would have to be prepared for a long struggle.

Initial reverses

After an initial clash at Mons, Belgium, the BEF retreated. It stood fast at Le Cateau on 26 August, but suffered heavy casualties. On 5 September the Battle of the Marne began, with the Germans only 48 kilometres from Paris. The battle raged for seven days – by 14 September the Germans had withdrawn to the River Aisne and Paris had been saved. In October each side tried to outflank the other – the so-called "race to the sea" merely extended the line of trenches. By the end of 1914 the trenches ran from the North Sea to Switzerland; the British section ran from Ypres in Belgium to the River Somme [1]. That 130-kilometre strip accounted for almost 90 per cent of the 2,883,000 casualties the war cost Britain.

By 1918 the four original divisions had grown to more than 60 and from 1916 onwards Britain increasingly became the dominant partner.

Under pressure from both Germany and Turkey, Russia appealed to the British at the end of 1914 for some action to distract the Turks. The result was the Gallipoli campaign [4] which lasted eight months, cost 100,000 British casualties, and ended in evacuation of the peninsula. While the Allies were on Gallipoli, Bulgaria joined the Central Powers. On 5 October 1915, in anticipation of an invasion of Serbia [2, 3], one British and one French division landed at Salonika, in neutral Greece. They finally moved in September 1918, forcing the Bulgarians to sign an armistice.

The desert campaign and war in Africa

The Mesopotamian campaign [4, 5] at first made good progress. Sent out from India to protect oil interests in Kuwait, a force under Gen. Charles Townshend (1861–1924) got to

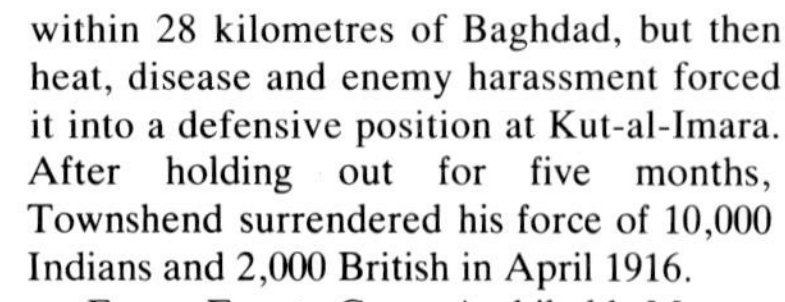

within 28 kilometres of Baghdad, but then heat, disease and enemy harassment forced it into a defensive position at Kut-al-Imara. After holding out for five months, Townshend surrendered his force of 10,000 Indians and 2,000 British in April 1916.

From Egypt Gen. Archibald Murray moved into the Sinai and by the end of 1916 was close to Gaza, the nearest point of Turkish-held Palestine. He was twice beaten back and in June 1917 was replaced by Gen. Sir Edmund Allenby (1861–1936). A month later Capt. T. E. Lawrence (1888–1935), with a force of Arabs, captured Akaba.

Baghdad had fallen to an army under Gen. Sir Stanley Maude (1864–1917) on 11 March 1917, at a cost of 92,500 casualties. Instead of reinforcing Gaza, the Turks decided to counter-attack at Baghdad, and Allenby mounted a two-pronged attack against Beersheba and Gaza. By 9 December he was in Jerusalem. There was then a prolonged pause. In September 1918 Allenby advanced again, sweeping up through Damascus to Aleppo; Gen. William Marshall (1865–1939), who had taken over after

CONNECTIONS

See also
What World War meant to Britain

In other volumes
Causes of World War I (31)
World War I (31)
The Peace of Paris (31)

1 British infantry had to endure trench-feet, lice, flies and monotonous rations as well as regular shellfire when in the trenches. Out of the line they spent their time in working parties. Combat consisted of small-scale raids into enemy trenches and large set-piece battles. In the Battle of the Somme in 1916 (this is the front line at Ovillers), there were 420,000 British casualties in four-and-a-half months.

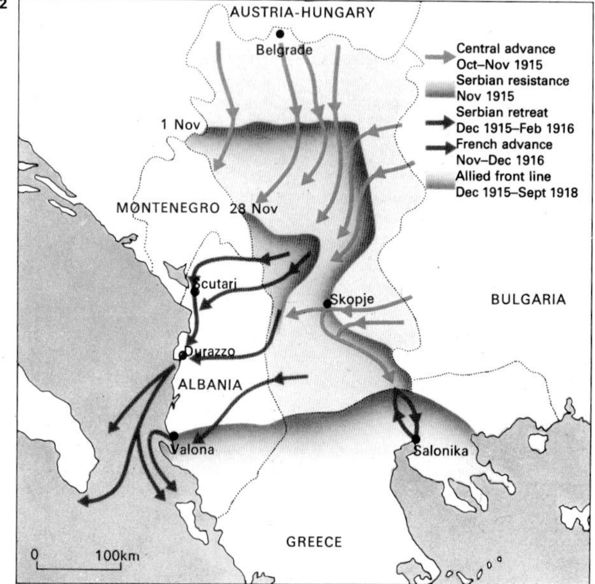

2 Serbia repulsed Austrian attacks three times in 1914. In October 1915 the Central Powers tried again, Austria and Germany attacking from the north and Bulgaria from the east. The Serbian army was forced to retreat across the Albanian mountains in appalling conditions. Of its 300,000 men, only 135,000 reached the Adriatic. Of 500,000 civilian refugees who accompanied the army, only 200,000 survived.

3 Belgrade was taken by the Austrians on 2 December 1914, but recaptured by Serbs under Gen. Radomir Putnik (1847–1917). Ten months later it finally fell. This painting by Oscar Laske shows the last day's resistance. One consequence of WWI was the creation, in 1918, of what became modern Yugoslavia.

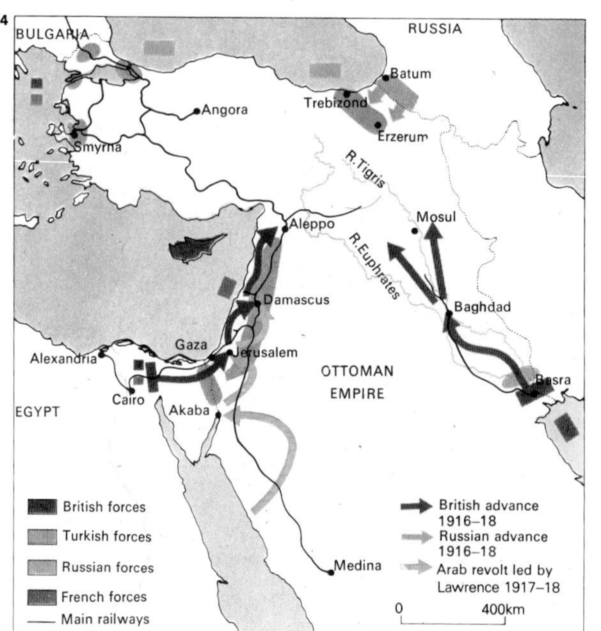

4 In the Middle East disease caused more casualties than enemy action. From January 1915 to the Armistice, 503,377 British troops went down with malaria, cholera, dysentery and other fevers, whereas only 51,500 were lost by enemy action. The eight-month campaign at Gallipoli in the Dardanelles, where the troops also suffered from disease, was an attempt to open a route to Russia via the Black Sea. An important consequence of its failure was that Russia was cut off from its foreign markets. One aspect of the desert war, later to be highly romanticized, was the exploits of T. E. Lawrence, who led an Arab revolt and led guerrilla raids against Turkish positions and the main railway.

Maude's death headed for Mosul. On 30 October Turkey surrendered.

Three weeks after the war began, a small British force accepted a German surrender in Togoland. In German Southwest Africa, Gen. Louis Botha (1862–1919), the Premier of the Union of South Africa, forced the Germans to surrender on 9 July 1915.

War in Europe

In August 1917 a decision by the German High Command to take the offensive on the Italian front [7] led to the Battle of Caporetto, fought between 24 October and 12 November. The Italians lost 305,000 men, 275,000 of whom surrendered, and five British divisions had to be pulled out of the Western Front and rushed to their support.

Cambrai, the first battle in which tanks were successfully used on a large scale, was yet another Allied attempt to break the deadlock that had existed since the beginning of 1915. In the three years since the Marne, the British had fought the First Battle of Ypres (October 1914, 58,000 casualties); Neuve-Chapelle (March 1915, 13,000); Second Ypres (April 1915, 59,000); Loos (September 1915, 60,000); the Somme (July-November 1916, 420,000); and Third Ypres (July-November 1917, 245,000).

The stalemate on land in those years had been offset to some extent by success at sea and in the air. The British blockade of Germany was extremely effective, whereas the German submarine campaign was restricted until late in 1916 by the fear of provoking the United States. When unrestricted submarine warfare was introduced, the British countered with the convoy system (the first sailed from Gibraltar on 10 May 1917) and improved anti-submarine technology. In the air, the Royal Flying Corps [6] received its first aircraft with synchronized guns in April 1916, and ended a ten-month period in which the German Air Services' 425 Fokker *Eindeckers* had created a reign of terror.

By 31 December 1917 there were 177,000 American troops in France, and less than a year later, at the Battle of Amiens (August 1918, 22,000 casualties) the end was in sight. At 11am on 11 November 1918 the shooting stopped.

KEY

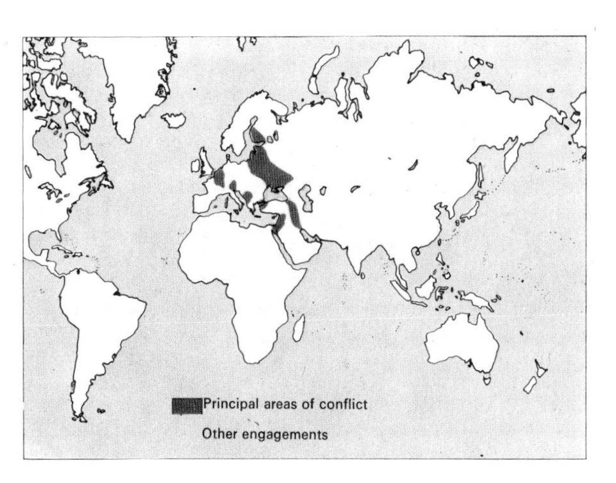

Britain's major concerns in WWI were France, Egypt, Gallipoli and Mesopotamia, but British and empire troops fought in the Pacific, Africa and even in China, where in November 1914 they joined the Japanese in the capture of Tsingtao. New Zealand took Samoa and Australia took New Guinea in the first two months; in November the raider *Emden* was sunk off the Cocos Islands. Other naval engagements included one at Dogger Bank in 1915, the historic Battle of Jutland in 1916, and the raid on the U-boats in Zeebrugge in 1918.

5

6

5 Australian and New Zealand cavalry, were part of Allenby's expedition to Gaza. The ANZACs (Australian and New Zealand Army Corps) also fought at Gallipoli, moving to the Western Front in 1916.

6 Captain Albert Ball, VC, was photographed in this SE5 at London Colney, Herts, in March 1917 and killed in it on 7 May. He was 20 years old. Ball shot down 44 German aircraft and, like Major Mick Mannock, VC, who with 73 victories was Britain's top World War I ace, was killed by machine-gun fire from the ground. The Royal Flying Corps sent 48 reconnaissance aircraft to France in 1914: by the end of the war the Royal Air Force (formed on 1 April 1918) had 22,171 serviceable aircraft. The war cost the air services 16,823 killed, of whom 12,782 were officers.

7

7 Italy joined the Allies in April 1915 and declared war on Austria-Hungary on 23 May 1915. Not until 1916 did it declare war on Germany. Many of the clashes between the Italians and the Austrians took place in the Alps: this Austrian gun is at a height of 3,860m (12,545ft). Of the five British divisions rushed to the Battle of Caporetto, two were withdrawn nine months later, but the troops who remained joined an Italian assault on the anniversary of Caporetto, in 1918, which led to the Austrians' seeking an armistice.

8

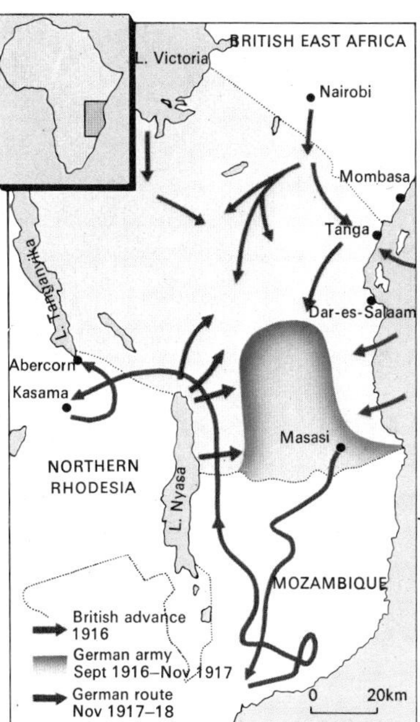

9

8 The East African campaign cost the British 19,000 casualties. That it was so protracted was due to the military genius of the German commander, Paul von Lettow-Vorbeck. who, with drastically outnumbered forces, fought on until November 1918.

9 Shorts and topees were standard uniform for troops in East Africa, and provided some relief from the intolerable heat. The torment of tsetse flies, fever and dysentery made conditions as bad, in their own way, as they were on the Western Front.

What World War I meant to Britain

World War I is seen as one of the turning-points in British history — but it would be wrong to suggest that before the war all was tranquillity and security, a last "golden age", and that after it all was uncertainty and depression. Major political, economic and social changes were already taking place in Britain and the empire before 1914. They would have overturned the old way of life anyway; the war merely speeded them up, and made their effects far more shattering than they would otherwise have been.

Optimism and disillusionment

In 1914, Britain had effectively been at peace for almost a century; the Crimean (1854–6) and Boer wars (1899–1902) had had little effect on the population, and had seemed only minor interruptions in the growth of Britain's power. Several generations had grown up who knew little of war and were convinced of the superiority of their country and race. But all levels of British society were becoming more aware of the German threat to British naval and commercial supremacy in the years before 1914, and the hostility that this caused goes some way towards explaining the enthusiasm with which war was greeted. More than 500,000 men volunteered in the first few weeks, and during the following year 125,000 men a month went gladly to the front [1].

Early hopes that the war would be over by Christmas 1914 faded as both sides dug in. A static war of attrition ensued. By mid-1916 the fighting men were disillusioned by the squalor of the trenches and the mass slaughter. Because new battalions were formed on a geographical basis, whole towns and villages in Britain were almost depopulated by the fighting. On 1 July 1916, the first day of the Battle of the Somme, nearly 20,000 British soldiers were killed: individual battalions suffered heavily, the 10th West Yorkshires, for example, losing almost 60 per cent of its strength. At home there were some shortages and a few air raids [4], but the civilian population never really understood what it was like at the front. At the start of the war the government established a Press Bureau with the task of censoring newspaper reports and the true progress of the war was concealed from the public. Instead, the mass of public opinion was coloured by propaganda stories of atrocities.

The economy and government control

The unforeseen demands that the war placed on the British economy forced the state to intervene more actively than ever before. Although attempts were made after the war to retreat from this, active state involvement was never lost. The need for vast supplies of munitions, and the inability of private industry to produce them, led to the creation of a Ministry of Munitions in May 1915 with considerable directive powers. In 1916 British Summer Time was introduced to prolong daylight working hours. The need to ensure adequate food supplies led, in December 1916, to the establishment of county committees to direct agriculture and the creation of a Ministry of Food. In 1918 rationing was introduced.

The war brought an end to the free trade policy that Britain had struggled to maintain since the 1840s. The McKenna duties of 1915, putting a tariff on luxury imports,

CONNECTIONS

See also
The fight for the vote
World War I: Britain's role
The British Labour Movement 1868-1930
British foreign policy since 1919
Britain 1930-45

In other volumes
World War I (31)
The Peace of Paris (31)
The twenties and the Depression (31)

1 Voluntary recruiting at first resulted in more men than could be adequately trained or equipped. The outbreak of war was greeted with overwhelming enthusiasm by all classes. Hatred of the Germans was whipped up by an almost hysterical press, and the chance of adventure and glory after long years of peace brought men flocking to join the forces. With no conscription, Britain had to rely on volunteers and, in spite of massive losses, the supply of new recruits was adequate for more than a year. But the authorities felt obliged to introduce conscription by May 1916 in order to reinforce the depleted ranks.

2 These women working in a factory in 1917 testify to the sexual revolution that took place on the home front during the war. As more and more men volunteered or were drafted into the forces, their places in the munitions factories, shops, offices, voluntary services, hospitals, schools and transport were taken by women. By thus ably replacing men or working beside them, women's claims for equality of status and rights were so widely accepted that in 1918 an Act giving the vote to women over the age of 30 was passed with very little opposition. After so many women had gained social and economic independence, there was no way for the conventional barriers to be re-erected once the war was over. This radical change in attitudes was reflected later, in the 1920s, in extremes of fashion and a degree of permissiveness in social behaviour

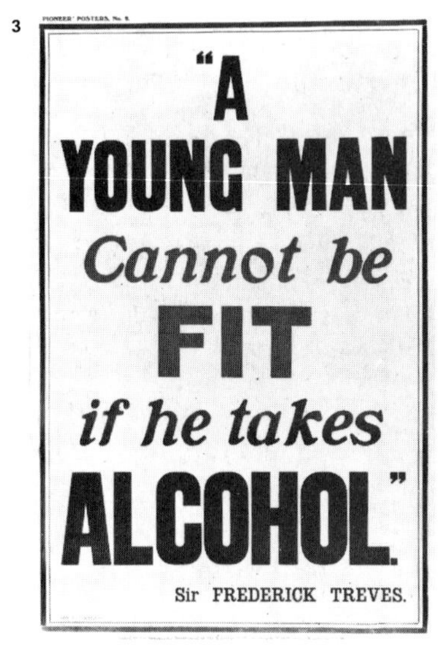

3 Watered beer and afternoon closing of the pubs were introduced by the government because it was felt that the national consumption of alcohol was impairing the war effort.

4 Barrage balloons, thinly spread over London, served as token protection rather than forming any serious deterrent to German air attacks. London was first bombed by Zeppelins (1915) but these were vulnerable and soon replaced by aeroplanes.

5 Wilfred Owen (1893-1918) and other young poets such as Siegfried Sassoon (1886-1967) and Robert Graves (1895-1985), who had fought in the trenches, wrote about the horror and despair of the experiences through which they had passed.

were retained after 1918, and were followed in 1921 by a Safeguarding of Industry Act to protect certain industries against foreign competition. On the outbreak of war, the Bank of England was authorized to issue banknotes not backed by gold, and there was a rapid and lasting rise in rates of income tax, which themselves had a much more progressive structure. The national debt rose from £650 million in 1914 to more than £7,000 million in 1918.

Shortages of labour caused by the demand for troops made workers realize their strength. Trade union membership rose from 4.1 million in 1913 to 6.5 million in 1918 and 8.3 million in 1920. Similarly, the widespread recruitment of women into industry broke down prejudices and strengthened the cause of the suffragettes [2]

The peacetime boom and slump

In November 1918 there was little evidence of any widespread demoralization caused by wartime losses – rather a pride in having come through an unprecedented trial. David Lloyd George (1863–1945), who had become prime minister of a Liberal-Tory coalition in 1916, took the opportunity to hold a general election which swept the coalition back into office. There was a brief restocking and rebuilding boom, but by spring 1920 it had degenerated into speculation and collapsed [6]. The economy slumped and the numbers of those unemployed rose to more than two million in June 1921 [8].

The government attempted to correct the economy by cutting public spending, wages and prices, all of which only made the problem worse. The war had accelerated the decline of Britain from the industrial and commercial supremacy it had once enjoyed. Traditional export markets had developed their own industries and major exporting sectors of the British economy, such as cotton, coal and shipping, were permanently reduced [7]. The war had given impetus to some new industries, such as chemicals and motor car manufacturing. But these tended to be developed in new regions, far from the traditional centres of industry where the misery and hopelessness of long-term unemployment were at their worst.

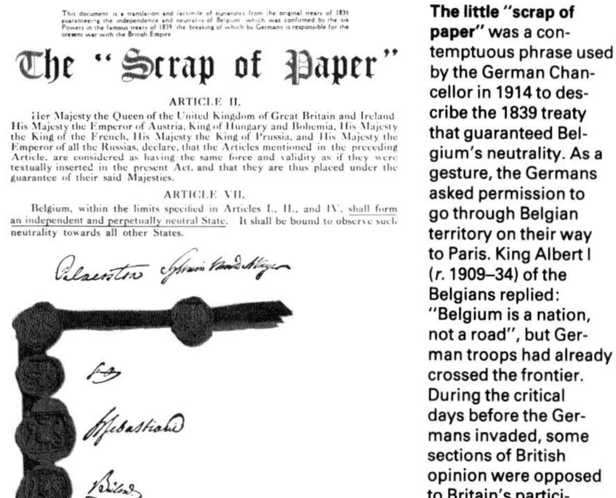

This document is a translation and facsimile of signatures from the original treaty of 1831 guaranteeing the independence and neutrality of Belgium, which was confirmed by the six Powers in the famous treaty of 1839, the breaking of which by Germany is responsible for the present war with the British Empire.

The "Scrap of Paper"

ARTICLE II.

Her Majesty the Queen of the United Kingdom of Great Britain and Ireland His Majesty the Emperor of Austria, King of Hungary and Bohemia, His Majesty the King of the French, His Majesty the King of Prussia, and His Majesty the Emperor of all the Russias, declare, that the Articles mentioned in the preceding Article, are considered as having the same force and validity as if they were textually inserted in the present Act, and that they are thus placed under the guarantee of their said Majesties.

ARTICLE VII.

Belgium, within the limits specified in Articles I., II., and IV., shall form an independent and perpetually neutral State. It shall be bound to observe such neutrality towards all other States.

PALMERSTON
British Plenipotentiary
SYLVAN VAN DE WEYER
Belgian Plenipotentiary
SENFFT
Austrian Plenipotentiary
H. SEBASTIANI
French Plenipotentiary
BULOW
Prussian Plenipotentiary
POZZO DI BORGO
Russian Plenipotentiary

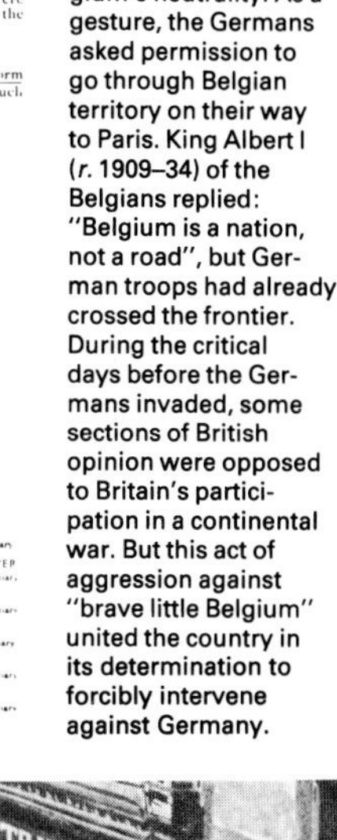

The little "scrap of paper" was a contemptuous phrase used by the German Chancellor in 1914 to describe the 1839 treaty that guaranteed Belgium's neutrality. As a gesture, the Germans asked permission to go through Belgian territory on their way to Paris. King Albert I (*r.* 1909–34) of the Belgians replied: "Belgium is a nation, not a road", but German troops had already crossed the frontier. During the critical days before the Germans invaded, some sections of British opinion were opposed to Britain's participation in a continental war. But this act of aggression against "brave little Belgium" united the country in its determination to forcibly intervene against Germany.

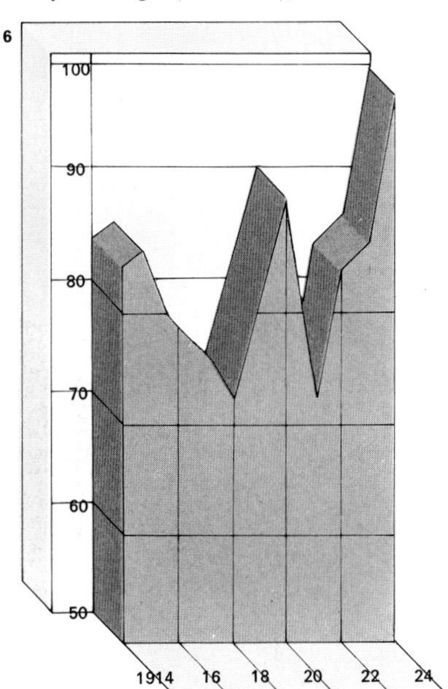

6 Britain's gross national product enjoyed a brief boom immediately after the war as industry restocked and changed over to peacetime products. But drastic cuts in government expenditure, the loss of export markets and the erosion of favourable economic conditions, such as free trade, led to a severe slump.

7
8,050
6,913
6,046
4,445
1912
1924
Production
Export
(million sq yds)

7 Cotton production and exports in the decade from 1912 to 1922 show a postwar slump that was typical of several major British industries. After the war they discovered that many of their markets had disappeared forever. It was a failure to replace the jobs in these industries that was the basic cause of lasting unemployment.

8

8 Unemployment was non-existent during the war, but after 1920 an intricate system of reliefs had to be built up in response to a fundamental change in the attitude of the public. Before the war the unemployed had been resigned to their fate as an inevitable fact of life. But after the war men expected the government to find them jobs, or to support them adequately until the necessary employment was available.

9 Ex-servicemen hawking their wares in the streets in 1920 symbolized the disillusionment and despair that broke down all the old certainties of British society. There was a dawning and bitter realization that the prodigious feats of government organization and direction that had helped to win the war did not seem to be winning the peace. The poor no longer accepted their fate as inevitable or unalterable, while the middle classes saw their income and status being steadily eroded by higher taxes. The frivolities of the "Gay Twenties" stemmed from a widespread desire to ignore doubts and difficulties that seemed insoluble. It amounted to enjoying life for the moment and letting tomorrow look after itself.

9

10

10 Striking coal miners in Wigan formed part of a "triple alliance" of miners, engineering and transport unions who were prepared to call a national strike. There was little industrial strife early in the war, but various government Acts, such as the Munitions of War Act of 1915 (which set wage levels and enforced arbitration), led to widespread strikes in 1917. The government modified its approach, but when in 1921 rising unemployment coincided with a withdrawal of government subsidies, support for a minimum wage, and removal of state control over the mines, the triple alliance was born. But the government compromised, the transport and engineering workers withdrew their support, and the threat of a general strike was ended. The miners came out alone, but within three months they were defeated, and returned under worse conditions than could have been reached by negotiation. This was followed by the political excitement over the collapse of Lloyd George's coalition government in October 1922.

The British Labour Movement 1868-1930

The driving force behind the British labour movement in the latter half of the nineteenth century was the trade unions, which had been given restricted legality in 1825. Until the advent of the so-called "new unionism" in the 1880s, most trade unions were associations of skilled workers of varying political allegiance. Nonetheless, by the 1880s they had established a relatively secure position for themselves. In 1871 trade unions had been given legal recognition and in 1875 peaceful picketing was legalized.

New unionism

The period from 1875 to 1900 saw rapid growth in trade unions. This resulted partly from the rising prestige of the Trades Union Congress (TUC) which was founded in 1868, and partly from the efforts of a generation of "new unionists" who preached a much more militant form of trade unionism and organized semi-skilled and unskilled workers, such as dockers and gas workers, into new, industrial unions [Key]. These unions were prepared to take strike action with much less hesitation than before [2]. The result was the growth of working-class solidarity, an increasing dissatisfaction with the Liberal Party and the spread of genuinely socialist ideas among working men.

The growth of socialism had been demonstrated in 1888 when James Keir Hardie (1856–1915) and R. B. Cunninghame Graham (1852–1936) founded the Scottish Labour Party. It was given national expression in 1893 when Hardie [3] founded the Independent Labour Party (ILP) with the aim of encouraging trade unionists and socialists to join forces for the creation of an independent political party with working-class representation in Parliament. A non-revolutionary path to socialism was also sought by the Fabian Society which was founded in 1884. Among its best known exponents were Sidney (1859–1947) and Beatrice (1858–1943) Webb and the writer George Bernard Shaw (1856–1950). In 1900 the Fabians, with the ILP, the Marxist Social Democratic Federation and trade unionists, set up the Labour Representation Committee (LRC). Its aim, to quote Hardie, was to form a distinct Labour group in Parliament. Its first secretary was James Ramsay Macdonald (1866–1937).

The LRC's programme was a moderate one – it avoided commitment either to socialism or to the class war. As a result, in 1901, it lost the support of the Marxist Federation, but it did gain considerable trade union support, largely in reaction to the Taff Vale decision by the House of Lords in 1901 which found trade unions liable for losses incurred through strikes. In 1906, therefore, the LRC saw 29 out of 50 of its candidates elected to Parliament; later that year, the LRC was renamed the Labour Party.

The growth of the Labour Party

From 1906 to 1914 the Labour Party supported the social reforms of the Liberal governments, which in turn passed legislation benefiting the trade unions. The Trade Dispute Act of 1906 reversed the Taff Vale decision of 1901 and the Trade Union Act in 1913 allowed trade unions to support the Labour Party financially. Nonetheless from 1910 to 1914 trade union militancy increased [4] as a result of rising prices and the spread,

CONNECTIONS

See also
The British Labour Movement to 1868
Social reform 1800-1914
The fight for the vote
Scotland in the 19th century
Britain 1930-45

In other volumes
Early socialism in the West (29)
The twenties and the Depression (31)

1 The London match girls came out on strike in 1888. Their appalling working conditions had previously been exposed by the Fabian lecturer Mrs Annie Besant (1847–1933) in her paper *The Link*. With her help and that of other socialists, the match girls were eventually victorious and won recognition for their union. This was one of the first examples of the wave of "new unionist" activity and organization that spread among the semi-skilled and unskilled workers from 1889. It clearly indicated the bad conditions that had to be endured by these people who made up by far, the bulk of the British working class.

2 The London dock strike (1889), the first major action of its kind by unskilled workers, lasted five weeks. It ended in victory for the dockers who won their claim for a basic 6d (2½p) an hour (the "dockers' tanner"). The most significant aspect of the strike, however, was the widespread support won by the dockers from skilled workers and other sectors of the community. The dockers advertised their case skilfully and thus notably advanced the cause of working-class solidarity. Their militancy also highlighted the spread of socialism among British workers.

3 James Keir Hardie was one of the leading and best-loved figures in the British labour movement. Born in Lanarkshire, Scotland, he worked as a coal miner from the age of ten, and in 1886 formed the Scottish Miners Federation. He was the first chairman of the Scottish Labour Party (1888), and in 1892 became the first workers' representative in Parliament when he was elected as an independent Labour MP. Through his tireless efforts he was involved in the foundation of the Independent Labour Party in 1893, and the Labour Representation Committee, in 1900. He lost his seat in 1895, but was re-elected in 1900 as Labour MP for Merthyr Tydfil, south Wales, which he held until his death.

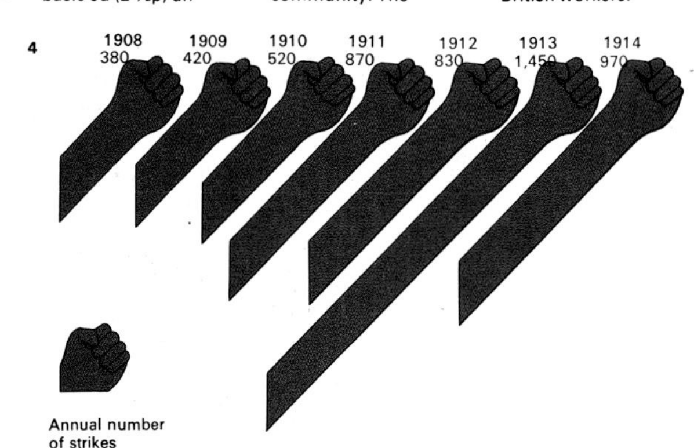

4 Industrial unrest characterized the years 1911–14. In 1908 there were 380 strikes; in 1913 there were 1,450. Dockers, seamen, railwaymen, and miners all struck between 1911 and 1914. There were militant and bitter conflicts and the men often held out for long periods in support of their demands. The strikes were prompted by various factors – the restoration of trade unions' legal immunity in 1906, falling standards of living, the apparent failure of the Labour Party to protect the interests of the working class, and the growth of Marxist and syndicalist ideas among working men. With the onset of the war in 1914, unrest declined because most union leaders and members chose to back the war effort.

from France and the United States, of syndicalist ideas that advocated a general strike to destroy capitalism.

The Labour Party continued to co-operate with the Liberal Party in Parliament and during World War I Arthur Henderson (1863–1935), who succeeded MacDonald as leader of the Labour Party in 1914, sat in the war cabinet of the coalition government. Various other Labour members also held administrative posts. By 1918, however, the Labour Party stood for a more independent policy, and influenced by events in Russia, adopted a more socialist constitution.

After the war the Labour Party soon became the second party in the country. Disillusionment, unemployment, and political strife within the Liberal Party meant that the Labour Party became the official opposition in Parliament in 1922. In 1924 Ramsay MacDonald became prime minister at the head of a minority government. His administration lasted only ten months. Publication of the so-called "Zinoviev letter" – instructions for a communist uprising in Britain apparently sent by Gregori Zinoviev (1883–1936), chairman of the Communist International – severely damaged the Labour Party. Although the letter was later proved to be forged, Labour fell before the Conservatives in November 1924.

The second Labour Government

In 1926 the trade unions challenged Conservative rule when the TUC supported the General Strike on behalf of the miners [7] but the government successfully resisted the challenge and in 1927 outlawed general strikes and attempted to reduce trade union subscriptions to the Labour Party.

In 1929, with the onset of the Depression, Labour returned to office with Ramsay MacDonald once again at the head of a minority government. His cabinet was divided over economic policy. Because socialist legislation was impossible in the midst of the economic slump, in 1931 MacDonald formed a coalition national government. In doing so he forfeited the support of the Labour Party, whose parliamentary representation dropped sharply in the 1931 general election.

THE RIGHT TO WORK
MANIFESTO.

FELLOW CITIZENS.–

UNEMPLOYMENT IS STILL ON THE INCREASE. No section of the workers are exempt. The official figures – published in September – show that very nearly 9 per cent. of the skilled workers of the country are workless. These figures – serious as they are – do not reveal the whole facts, since they do not include the greater mass of suffering men and women – the unorganised and unskilled workers.

NEITHER THE CENTRAL GOVERNMENT NOR THE LOCAL AUTHORITIES ARE TAKING EFFECTIVE STEPS to meet this desperate condition of affairs. Theirs is a policy of "wait."

UNDER THESE CIRCUMSTANCES, we once more call upon the people everywhere – those in work, as well as the workless – to make their voices heard and their presence felt. Statistics and facts do not move the official mind. It is time, therefore, that the workers of the nation roused the Government with that historic utterance of the late Sir Henry Campbell-Bannerman: "Stop your fooling and get to business."

PARLIAMENT WILL MEET IN OCTOBER. Before that time, every member must be made to understand by his constituents that his first duty at the opening of the Session is to insist upon the immediate amendment of the Unemployed Workmen Act, 1905, which is a mockery and a delusion for those who are suffering, and an excuse for inaction by politicians.

THE ACT MUST BE MADE COMPULSORY, so as to place upon the State the responsibility of providing work with adequate financial support.

IF IT IS A QUESTION OF COERCION FOR IRELAND, money for a war, or for battleships Parliament can find it, and pass Acts in less than 24 hours. The demands of the starving unemployed deserve as prompt action.

SUFFER NO LONGER IN SILENCE. You have rights, and the most sacred right of all is your right to earn a honest living for yourselves and families.

TO COMPEL THE GOVERNMENT to recognise this right you must–

1. ORGANISE – Let those who are in work come to the rescue of those who are workless. It may be your turn next. Call upon the Local Distress Committee to open at once the Unemployed Registers. Form representative and determined deputations and wait upon the local authorities. Insist upon something being done and done quickly.

2. DEMONSTRATE – Bring the unemployed out into the open, in order to convince the public of their desperate need.

3. CALL UPON THE RELIGIOUS BODIES of the nation to support the agitation for the right to work and the right to live, since only by so doing can they justify their professions.

REMEMBER!

Governments help more quickly those who show that they are ready to help themselves. The silence of the Unemployed means the neglect of their needs. Therefore, we call upon every right-thinking man and woman to join with us in our attempt to put an end to those terrible conditions of life – hunger, cold and homelessness – to which Unemployment condemns so many of our fellow men with their wives and little children.

SIGNED ON BEHALF OF THE RIGHT TO WORK NATIONAL COUNCIL.

GEO. N. BARNES (Chairman)
J. KEIR HARDIE
J. RAMSAY MACDONALD
GEORGE LANSBURY, Treasurer.

MARY R. MACARTHUR
ANNIE COBDEN SANDERSON
EDWARD R. PEASE
HARRY QUELCH } Executive.
FRANK SMITH, Hon. Sec., 18, Clifford's Inn, London, E.C.

All who are in earnest in this locality should communicate with–

By the 1870s trade unions had achieved legal recognition. Until that time unions had followed no specific political viewpoint, but from the 1880s the movement took a new turn. Disillusioned with the Liberal Party and influenced by socialist ideas, the "new unions" increasingly stressed the political role. They demanded a legal minimum wage, an 8-hour day, and the right to work. Although union militancy continued until well after World War I – until its defeat in the General Strike of 1926 – with the establishment of the Labour Party by 1906 union activity increasingly followed more conventional, parliamentary channels.

5

5 Tom Mann (1856–1941) was one of the leading "new unionists" of the late 19th century. In 1881 he joined the Amalgamated Society of Engineers and by 1886 had become involved in the socialist movement. In that year he published a pamphlet arguing that a more militant attitude should be taken by trade unionists. In 1889 Mann helped to organize the London dock strike and from 1894–7 was secretary of the Independent Labour Party. He emigrated, and in 1902 was active in the Australian labour movement. In the 1920s, after his return to England, he became a founder of the British Communist Party, feeling that the existing unions could not be militant enough.

6

6 Labour exchanges were introduced into Britain in 1910 by Winston Churchill (1874–1965), then Liberal President of the Board of Trade. Advocated by the Poor Law commission of 1909 and by the economist William Beveridge (1879–1963), labour exchanges were intended to provide a service for workers seeking employment and for employers seeking labour. They also prepared the way for a national system of social insurance. Initially, they were not as effective as had been hoped. Registration of unemployment was not compulsory so that only one-third of vacancies were filled through the nationwide exchanges.

7

7 The 1926 General Strike lasted nine days (4–12 May). In the face of government resistance the Trades Union Congress ended the strike. The miners held out, in vain, until August.

8

8 Ramsay MacDonald was the Labour Party's first prime minister. In 1894 he joined the Independent Labour Party and was its chairman from 1906 to 1909. He helped to found the Labour Representation Committee and in 1924 became the first Labour Party premier. In 1929 he again became prime minister but was rejected by the Labour Party when he formed a coalition national government in 1931, the only way he saw of keeping Labour in power.

British foreign policy since 1914

Britain's aim in World War I (1914–18) – to prevent the domination of Europe by any single power – was achieved by the peace treaties imposed in 1919 on Germany and its allies. But then the Allied coalition that won the war dissolved: the United States withdrew into isolation, Russia, under communist control, campaigned against the West, and France disagreed with Britain on the treatment of Germany [1]. Between 1925 and 1930 British governments welcomed a short-lived reconciliation between France and Germany, helped by the flow of American money into Europe. But by 1931 the world was hit by a grave economic crisis.

The age of appeasement

The economic slump propelled Adolf Hitler (1889–1945), leader of the National Socialists, into power in Germany in 1933 and ended the liberal regime in Japan. This provided Britain with two major foreign-policy problems in the 1930s: the satisfaction of German pressure for revision of the Treaty of Versailles 1919, especially its reparation and disarmament clauses, and the expansion of Japanese militarists into Manchuria, which they annexed in all but name in 1931–2, and into China proper in 1933–7.

Britain was handicapped in dealing with these problems by three factors: First its economic weakness, expressed in long-term unemployment; second, a public opinion stunned by the losses in World War I and nervous about rearmament; finally the sheer inability of Britain and France, with no help from isolationist America, to control Germany and Japan, as well as a restless Italy under Benito Mussolini (1883–1945).

A confrontation became unavoidable after the Munich Agreement in September 1938 [5]. Britain and France thereby agreed to German occupation of the Sudetenland, which was Czech territory, accepting that this was Hitler's "final" demand; but on 15 March 1939 German forces cynically abrogated the agreement by taking over the rest of Czechoslovakia. Almost the only benefit derived by Britain from this short-sighted policy of appeasement was time to build up its pitiably weak defences. When Hitler confidently invaded Poland on 1 September 1939, the British government finally honoured their treaty obligations and declared war on Germany two days later.

Policy during World War II

After the collapse of France in June 1940, Britain faced Hitler's Europe alone. The military situation was transformed when Germany invaded the Soviet Union on 22 June 1941 and when the United States entered the war after the Japanese attack at Pearl Harbor on 7 December 1941. But the diplomatic situation was complicated. The United States' President, Franklin Roosevelt (1882–1945) agreed with the British Prime Minister, Winston Churchill (1874–1965) on general war aims in the Atlantic Charter, signed in August 1941, but had no interest in preserving the British Empire. At the Yalta conference (4–11 February 1945) the two met Soviet leader Joseph Stalin (1879–1953) and Roosevelt seemed to side with Stalin on imperial questions against the British.

Churchill, an old opponent of communism, willingly accepted Stalin's territorial claims in eastern Europe, but he was worried

CONNECTIONS

See also
British foreign policy 1815-1914
What World War I meant to Britain
Britain 1930-45
Britain since 1945: 1
Britain since 1945: 2

In other volumes
The Commonwealth (23)
The division of Europe (29)
Evolution of the Western democracies (29)
Europe from confrontation to glasnost (29)
The Peace of Paris (31)
East Asia 1919-45 (31)
Causes of World War II (31)
World War II (31)

1

1 On 11 January 1923, French and Belgian forces, despite British protests, occupied the German industrial Ruhr (until August 1925) as a penalty for alleged non-payment by Germany of coal reparations. In the aftermath of World War I, Britain and France disagreed over the treatment of Germany. Britain, intent upon economic recovery, wanted Germany leniently treated; France demanded strict enforcement of the Treaty of Versailles.

2

2 At the League of Nations, Geneva, in March 1925, Britain rejected a major attempt to enforce the peaceful settlement of international disputes in refusing to sign the Geneva Protocol. France sought to strengthen the League's powers of collective action against aggression by providing for compulsory arbitration of disputes. But Britain was wary of the protocol's absolute commitment to armed intervention.

3

3 Winston Churchill was a backbench MP during the 1930s, and an outspoken critic of the National Government's policy of appeasement towards Germany. Public opinion favoured a vague pacifism in the face of German rearmament and growing Italian and German aggression. Such was the desire for, if not faith in, peace, that British rearmament did not seriously begin until after 1938.

4

4 The Spanish Civil War was fought between the Nationalist rebels on the one hand, helped by Hitler and Mussolini, and the Spanish Republican Government on the other, from 1936 to 1939. The war seems to have presaged the later conflict waged between Fascism and democracy in World War II. But in 1936, the British Government was chief sponsor of an international agreement for non-intervention which was signed by all the major powers. This was adhered to by all countries except Italy, Germany and the Soviet Union – the last-named sent some aid to the Republican forces. Public opinion in Britain was divided: some, illegally, went to Spain to fight, mostly for the Republicans, whose British International Brigade numbered about 2,000 men.

5

5 The Munich Agreement of 29 September 1938 typified Britain's policy of appeasement. Britain, France and Italy agreed that the Sudeten region of Czechoslovakia should be ceded to Germany. British Prime Minister Neville Chamberlain (1869–1940), shown here on his return from Munich, made an agreement with Hitler to consult on any future Anglo-German questions. A year later Britain and Germany were at war.

how far into western Europe Soviet influence would penetrate, and whether the USA would help to resist it.

Postwar developments

In the immediate postwar period, Britain aimed to continue playing a world role, stay a close partner with the USA and provide leadership in the reconstruction of Europe. Beginning in 1947 (with independence being granted to India and Pakistan), the empire began to be dismantled.

The Labour government of 1945-51 hoped for co-operation between the Soviet Union and the West after the war but, as the East-West "cold war" developed, Labour ministers took Britain into the Brussels collective defence pact of 1948, and then into the North Atlantic Treaty Organization (NATO). This came into being in April 1949 with Canada, the USA and nine other western European states.

Britain's declining power and limited independence of action was shown in 1956. The British decision to occupy the Suez Canal zone in Egypt (with French and Israeli troops) after Nasser's nationalization of the canal [7] proved a disaster and US pressure forced the troops' withdrawal. In 1968, the Labour government's decision to withdraw military forces from east of Suez made clear that Britain would no longer underwrite commitments around the world.

On 1 January 1973 Britain entered the European Economic Community (now European Community [EC]). British commitment to Europe has been chequered, although she is a member of the Council of Europe and the Organization for Economic Co-operation and Development (OECD).

Two remaining colonies were to affect Britain's foreign policy in the 1980s. On 2 April 1982 Argentina invaded the Falkland Islands in the South Atlantic. Britain sent a naval task force and, after six weeks of fighting, regained the islands. In 1984, the British prime minister Margaret Thatcher (1925-) visited China to sign an agreement outlining the terms under which Hong Kong would become a special administrative region of China once the lease on the New Territories expired in 1997 [6].

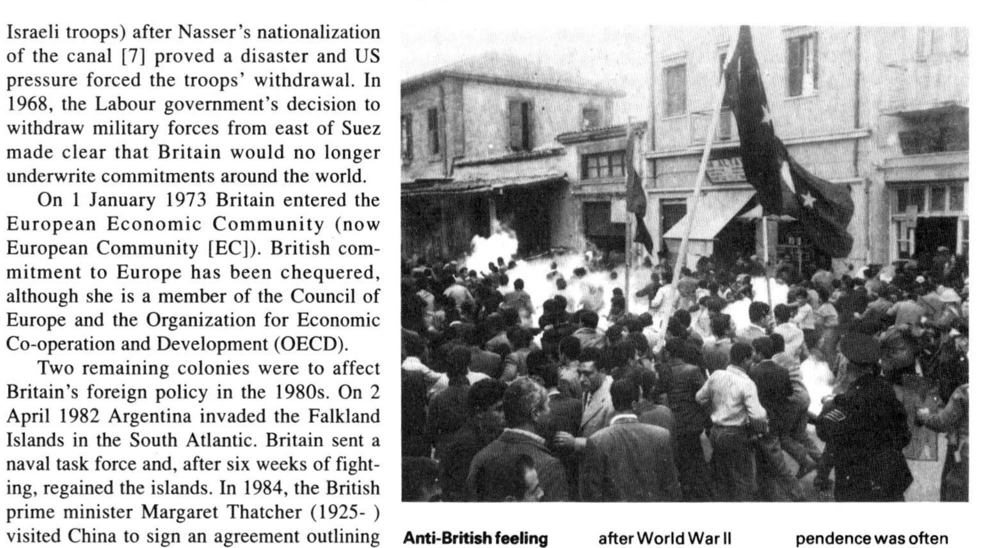

Anti-British feeling in Cyprus (1955–60) typified the strains of decolonization in areas where Britain's handover of power after World War II was complicated by divisions in the local community. In other colonies, the transition to independence was often peaceful. But areas of violence included mandated Palestine, India, Egypt, Kenya, Malaya and Aden.

6 British prime minister, Margaret Thatcher and Chinese premier Zhao Ziyang sign the "Hong Kong agreement" in 1984. Hong Kong has been a British crown colony since the 19th century. The lease under which this arrangement operated expires in 1997 and after this date, Hong Kong will become a special administrative region of China. The agreement outlines the conditions under which this new arrangement will operate.

7 The nationalization of the Suez Canal in July 1956 by Egypt's President Nasser provoked British and French fears that petroleum shipments between the Persian Gulf and western Europe would be cut off. Diplomatic efforts to settle the crisis failed, and Britain and France used the pretext of an Israeli invasion to seize the Canal by force. The troops seen here landed in November, but after US pressure a ceasefire took place within two days. The incident was a major blow to the international prestige of Britain and France. Anthony Eden (1897-1977) who had pressed for the use of force resigned as British prime minister the following January.

8 The Anglo-American "special relationship" was a principal feature of British foreign policy after 1945. Two of its chief exponents were Harold Macmillan (1894–1986) (left), the British Prime Minister (1957–63) and John F. Kennedy (1917–63) (right), US President (1961–63). Here they are shown after talks in Washington in 1961 that were aimed at controlling the spread of the H-bomb and increasing unity among the countries of the Western alliance.

9 The opening of the Zimbabwe/ Rhodesia constitutional conference at London's Lancaster House in September 1979. The talks were attended by the various factions in Zimbabwe/ Rhodesia, including Abel Muzorewa, Robert Mugabe, Joshua Nkomo and Ian Smith, and were chaired by Lord Carrington. The talks determined the terms of the interim constitution for an independent Zimbabwe.

10 The leaders of France and Britain, Georges Pompidou (1911-74), [right] and Edward Heath (1916–) [left] cleared the way for Britain to enter the EEC, in January 1973. When the Community was first formed in 1957 Britain refused to join, fearing the EEC's supranational powers. Two subsequent applications for membership, in 1961 and 1967, were both blocked by Pompidou's predecessor, President De Gaulle. Final talks had begun after De Gaulle's resignation, in 1969.

Britain 1930-45

Between 1930 and 1945 Britain experienced the deepest economic depression in its history and the massive mobilization of resources required for total war. In 1929, when a Labour government was elected under Ramsay MacDonald (1866–1937), Britain was already suffering from depression in its staple heavy industries: coal mining, iron and steel, textiles and shipbuilding.

Consequences of the Depression

The Labour government was pledged to tackle the problem of unemployment, which stood at more than one million [1]. No sooner was the government formed, however, than the Wall Street Crash (1929) in the USA plunged the major western industrial economies into deeper depression. By 1931 the government was faced with more than two-and-a-half million unemployed and a heavy drain on its resources to meet the cost of unemployment benefits. The Labour government had little to offer as a solution to the economic depression. Radical voices, such as that of Oswald Mosley (1896-1980), a junior member of the Labour government, and Lloyd George (1863–1945), leader of the Liberals, offered solutions along the lines later advocated by John Maynard Keynes (1883–1946), but were ignored in the pursuit of orthodox economic policy. This dictated that the government should curtail its expenditure and raise business confidence in the hope that normal trading conditions would begin to reduce unemployment. The recommended cuts in expenditure included a reduction in unemployment benefit.

In 1931, the Labour cabinet was deeply divided over implementing the cuts. The government was forced to resign over the issue, but MacDonald and a group of Labour MPs joined with the Conservatives and Liberals to form a coalition, the National Government. A general election was then called, which led to a resounding victory for the new administration.

The National Government introduced cuts in government expenditure, especially in unemployment benefit and the pay of state employees such as teachers and civil servants. Gradually the coalition was converted into a Conservative administration which triumphed at the general election of 1935.

In spite of the absence of major economic initiatives from governments in office after 1931, the economic situation began to improve from 1933 onwards. Unemployment reached a peak of almost three million in the winter of 1932–3 and remained at more than a million until the outbreak of war in 1939, but it was falling from 1933–4. Revival was concentrated in a range of new industries such as electricity supply, motor vehicles [2], consumer durables and chemicals. These industries brought increased employment to the southeast and the Midlands, while the older industries of the "distressed" areas remained depressed and only slowly began to recover.

Political unrest and social change

The rise in prosperity in some areas helps to explain the failure of the extremist parties to obtain greater support before the war. Oswald Mosley [8] formed the British Union of Fascists in 1932, after leaving the Labour Party and adopted the style of continental fascist parties. The party espoused radical

CONNECTIONS

See also
British foreign policy since 1919

In other volumes
Stalin's Russia (29)
Early socialism in the West (29)
The rise of fascism (29)
The Peace of Paris (31)
The twenties and the Depression (31)
World War II (31)

1

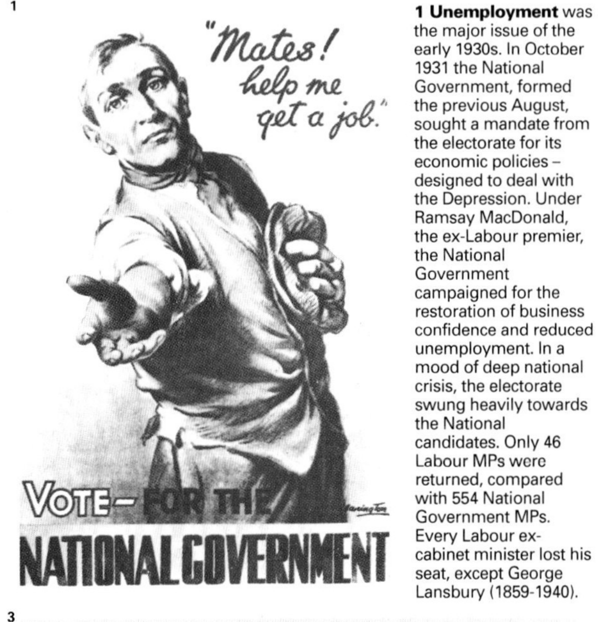

1 Unemployment was the major issue of the early 1930s. In October 1931 the National Government, formed the previous August, sought a mandate from the electorate for its economic policies – designed to deal with the Depression. Under Ramsay MacDonald, the ex-Labour premier, the National Government campaigned for the restoration of business confidence and reduced unemployment. In a mood of deep national crisis, the electorate swung heavily towards the National candidates. Only 46 Labour MPs were returned, compared with 554 National Government MPs. Every Labour ex-cabinet minister lost his seat, except George Lansbury (1859-1940).

2

2 Mass production methods, pioneered in the United States, were adopted in Britain during the interwar years. They brought the first cheap motor vehicles within the reach of the middle classes. By 1939 there were nearly two million motor vehicles in Britain and the "motoring revolution" had begun. Car production for the home market increased each year up to the war, with the exception of 1932.

3

3 The communist-led National Unemployed Workers' Movement organized several "hunger" marches on London in the thirties to protest about the plight of the unemployed. The marches however, had little effect on government policy.

4

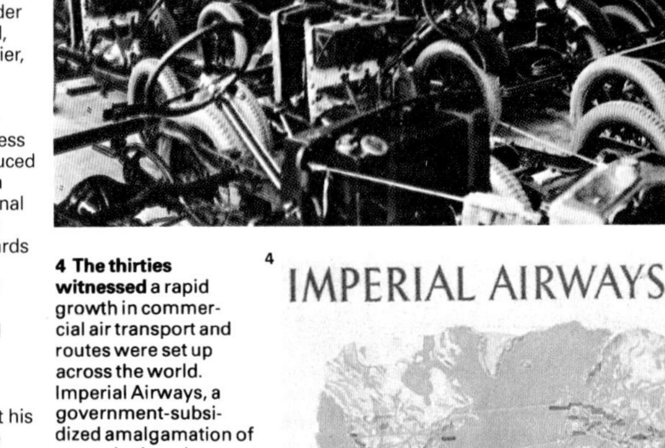

4 The thirties witnessed a rapid growth in commercial air transport and routes were set up across the world. Imperial Airways, a government-subsidized amalgamation of several privately-owned companies, was established in 1924. One of its main aims was to routes throughout the empire. Airmail was as important as passenger services; by 1938 Imperial Airways carried all first-class mail to the empire.

5

5 Private house building expanded greatly in the 1930s, and was a principal factor in the economic recovery during the last half of the decade. Despite government cuts in building programmes, private investment in housing boomed, especially in the thriving regions of the Midlands and the south-east. Nearly three million houses were built between 1930 and 1939. This expansion in building led to a boom in other industries such as electrical and household goods.

economic ideas but earned a reputation for violence and anti-semitism that cut it off from mass support.

The thirties witnessed the rise of new social patterns, with an enormous growth of suburban living, a housing boom [5], slum clearance, and ameliorative social legislation. Opportunities for leisure activities, such as the cinema [6] and dance halls, expanded and provided cheap entertainment. Another influencial and inexpensive source of entertainment was the radio. The BBC broadcast hours of popular music daily and did much to enhance the reputations of some of the great dance bands of the 1930s. The rise of the football pools, with their lure of instant wealth, was another social phenomenon of the times.

There was a profound distrust and loathing of war in the thirties. Peace movements flourished and the governments of Stanley Baldwin (1867-1947) and Neville Chamberlain (1869-1940) pursued a policy of appeasing the dictators. But rising international tension led to gradual rearmament from the mid-1930s, helping to revive the economy.

The experiences of the Depression and thirties followed by total war helped to create a new mood in Britain. The Beveridge Report of 1942 advocated a high level of employment and the creation of a welfare state. Even before the end of the war, the Butler Education Act of 1944 made free secondary education available to all.

Postwar optimism

World War II witnessed an acceleration of many of the trends evident in British politics and society before 1939. The war further stimulated new industries as well as reviving the old ones, and led to widespread recognition of social problems such as poverty and unemployment. Labour's programme for industrial nationalization and extension of social services paved the way for its victory at the 1945 general election. The Labour government inherited considerable good will from the electorate. Demobilization caused far less resentment than it had in 1918 [10] and Labour's programme seemed to meet the demand for new policies and an avoidance of mass unemployment.

Edward VIII (1894–1972), came to the throne on 20 January 1936, with considerable popular support, accumulated during his years as Prince of Wales. Public interest in his life showed the widespread devotion to the monarchy even during the worst years of the Depression. But the King's continuing relationship with an American divorcee, Mrs Wallace Simpson (1896–1986), precipitated a constitutional crisis following her second divorce in October 1936. The King wanted to marry her, but the Prime Minister, Stanley Baldwin (1867–1947), advised that she was unacceptable as Queen. In spite of considerable popular support for Edward, he abdicated in December.

6

6 The cinema was one of the most important forms of cheap mass entertainment in the 1930s. By 1939 there were 5,000 cinemas in Britain and more than 20 million cinema tickets were sold each week.

7

7 Rising living standards for those in work as well as a more widespread introduction of paid holidays contributed to a growth in holiday-making. The first holiday camps were opened in 1937.

8

8 Oswald Mosley's British Union of Fascists held many demonstrations and marches in the years before the war. Their use of uniforms and violent methods aroused widespread hostility, as did, more particularly, their anti-semitism. In 1936 the Public Order Act was passed forbidding the use of uniforms and strengthening police powers against political demonstrations and mass meetings.

9

9 Britain was slow to rearm in the thirties. Limited rearmament was undertaken from 1934, mainly in the airforce and navy, although German expenditure on arms was sometimes exaggerated. The government delayed thoroughgoing rearmament until after 1938 on the assumption that public opinion, as manifested in the Peace Ballot (a house-to-house poll) and by-election results, would not stand for sterner measures.

10

10 The immense war-effort in Britain put eight million people into uniform in World War II. Over 300,000 members of the armed forces and, on the home front, about 60,000 civilians lost their lives in the conflict. In contrast with 1919, demobilization went relatively smoothly, although in the Far and Middle East, British troops often became involved in local police-keeping and occupation duties, such as in Cyprus, that continued for some time after 1945.

World War II: Britain's role

Britain's involvement in World War II was global. Though its principal areas of concern were Europe, North Africa and the Far East, the Royal Air Force flew missions on the Russian front and Royal Navy ships fought engagements off South America. And where Britain itself was not heavily involved – notably in the Pacific theatre – Australians and New Zealanders fought alongside Britain's American allies.

Early campaigns

In May 1940, eight months after invading Poland, the Germans swept into Holland, Belgium and then France [1]. Heading for the English Channel, they forced a British Expeditionary Force (BEF) of 10 divisions back to Dunkirk. Miraculously, all but 25,000 to 30,000 men were rescued by a flotilla of small craft from Britain. In their flight, the BEF had to leave behind all heavy weapons.

After France fell, the Battle of Britain opened in early July with sorties by Goering's Luftwaffe against shipping and South Coast ports. On 10 July, Germany attacked convoys in the Straits of Dover. Phase two, which began on "Eagle Day", 13 August, was aimed at RAF fighter bases in Kent. On 7 September, having lost 225 aircraft to the RAFs 185 in just eight days, the Luftwaffe turned aside to attack London. On 15 September – "Battle of Britain Day" – it lost between 56 and 60 aircraft to the RAF's 26. Chastened, Goering switched to night attacks against English cities, and Operation Sea Lion, the invasion of Britain, was first postponed and finally abandoned altogether after the invasion of Russia. The blitz, during which some 30,000 people were killed, continued until mid-April 1941.

The dark days

A consequence of the fall of France was that the German navy was able to operate U-boats from France's west coast. In the first year of the war the U-boats never numbered more than 60, but they sank nearly a million tonnes of merchant shipping. The Battle of the Atlantic reached its peak in early 1941, but by the summer of 1943, the convoy system and American involvement prevailed.

In the Balkans Hitler's seven-week campaign through Yugoslavia and Greece ended with the British being ejected from Crete [2] in May 1941.

Germany's assault on Russia on 22 June 1941 [4] offered Britain a breathing-space. Britain could do little to help Russia beyond offering supplies: and the route to Murmansk and Archangel was, in the winter, the worst sea-route in the world.

While the Battle of the Atlantic and of the Russian convoys was under way, Britain was losing in the Far East. The Japanese attack on the US base at Pearl Harbor on 7 December 1941 was followed by the ignominious fall of Singapore [5], the loss of the battle cruiser *Repulse* and the battleship *Prince of Wales*, and a threat to India. The Japanese were within 320 kilometres of Australia; Australia and New Zealand, with most of their troops in North Africa, had to turn to the USA for protection.

Towards final victory

The tide began to turn in 1942. In North Africa, after a see-saw series of battles in which the Italians and Erwin Rommel's

CONNECTIONS

See also
Britain 1930-45
The home front in World War II

In other volumes
Stalin's Russia (29)
The rise of fascism (29)
The division of Europe (29)
The Peace of Paris (31)
East Asia 1919-45 (31)
Causes of World War II (31)
World War II (31)
Australia since 1918 (31)
New Zealand since 1918 (31)

1 The Allies and Germany faced each other in the West at the outbreak of war more or less evenly matched in numbers. Britain and France had 122 divisions against Germany's 136, and 3,254 armoured vehicles against 2,574. But the Allies still pursued outmoded ideas of positional warfare, and made poor use of their armoured divisions. German armour was used to optimum advantage and coupled with air power to form the spearhead of the *Blitzkrieg*. This was designed to burst through and surround the enemy rather than fight head-on battles. As a result Paris fell in only four weeks.

2 German paratroops, here entering a JU52 transport aircraft, proved decisive in the capture of Crete, the final phase of Hitler's Balkan campaign. Bernard Freyberg (1889–1963), commander of the New Zealand Division, was in charge of all the forces on the island. Using 1,390 aircraft, the Germans forced the British to withdraw on 27 May, after three weeks' stubborn resistance.

3 The arrival of Erwin Rommel (1891–1944) and his Afrika Korps in February 1941 rescued his Italian partners from being completely overrun by British and Commonwealth forces in North Africa. Twice Rommel reached the frontiers of Egypt, engendering Allied nightmares of an Axis victory that, together with an advance in the Caucasus, could have completed a successful pincer movement.

4 Hitler's invasion of the Soviet Union began brilliantly with the German armies using tactics that had been perfected in Poland and France. Deep-thrusting columns destroyed more than a million enemy troops, but stiffening Soviet resistance and the onset of merciless winter conditions prevented the Germans from achieving the swift victory they needed. Despite some further successes in 1942, the Germans were catastrophically defeated at Stalingrad where they lost 300,000 men. Thereafter they could not hope to match the Soviet Union's apparently inexhaustible manpower and were steadily pushed back.

5 The Japanese captured 85,000 men at Singapore in February 1942: it was the largest surrender in the history of the British Army. Complacency about the Japanese threat had led Britain to neglect already inadequate defences, but even so British and Commonwealth troops outnumbered the Japanese who swept through Malaya and Burma. The Japanese relied on their mastery of jungle warfare to outflank British troops, who had virtually no jungle training. Singapore was approached and attacked from its lightly defended landward side and fell in a matter of days.

Afrika Korps [3] got to within 96 kilometres of Alexandria, and Australian and British units distinguished themselves by stubborn resistance in the isolated pocket of Tobruk, Montgomery won the Battle of El Alamein [6]. The battle opened on 23 October; on 4 November Rommel's Afrika Korps began to retreat; four days later Anglo-American forces landed in French North Africa. With victory in North Africa in the spring of 1943, Italy became the next objective. Sicily was invaded in July 1943 and mainland Italy – by the British 5th Army at Salerno – in September. American insistence that the Pacific and Burma campaigns be given priority in late 1943 meant, however, that the Italian campaign was drawn out. Of the Commonwealth troops who had fought in Africa, the New Zealanders went on to fight in Italy, notably at Monte Cassino [7] and the Australians returned home to help push the Japanese out of the Pacific.

The Mediterranean campaign ended effectively with the capture of Rome on 4 June 1944, although the German resistance in Italy did not end until May 1945.

The invasion of Normandy began on 6 June 1944, British troops landing on the coast near Caen and Bayeux and Americans farther west. After an initial period of close fighting in France, the Allies broke out and swept towards the Rhine. An attempt to speed matters by an airborne landing at Arnhem in The Netherlands [8] failed, but in the spring of 1945 renewed offensives resulted in Germany's surrender on 7 May.

In the Far East Slim's [9] "forgotten" 14th Army had been confronting the Japanese in Burma while Americans, Australians and New Zealanders island-hopped towards Japan following the Battle of Midway, an American carrier-fleet victory that ranked with Stalingrad in strategic importance. Two atomic bombs, on Hiroshima and Nagasaki, ended the war against Japan.

Britain lost far fewer men in World War II than in World War I – 300,000 dead against 750,000. Civilian casualties were higher: 60,000 against 1,500. The legacy of the war was an enormous economic debt – £4,198 million – the loss of an empire and, in compensation, an industrial leap forward.

KEY

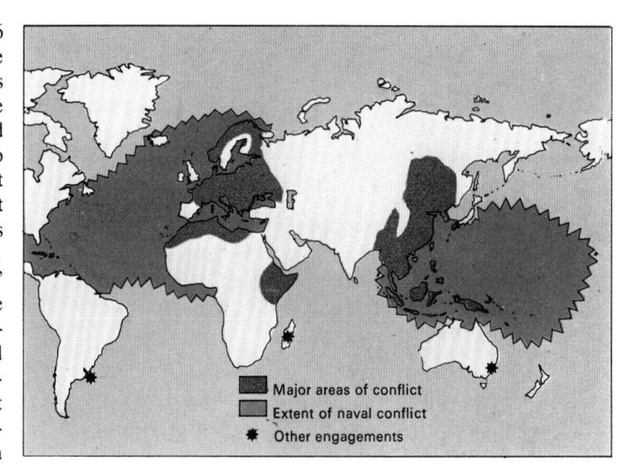

World War II began in Europe, but developed into a global conflict with campaigns in Africa, Asia and throughout the Pacific and Atlantic Oceans. Italy proved a weak member of the Axis in 1940, but Germany and Japan enjoyed a series of victories in the first three years. Thereafter, Allied superiority in potential manpower and industrial capacity steadily grew. More than any previous conflict, this was a war of technology, with developments in tanks, aircraft, submarines, radar – and eventually the atomic bomb – helping to influence strategic and tactical thinking.

6

6 The turning-point in North Africa came in July 1942 when the overstretched Afrika Korps failed to break through British 8th Army positions around El Alamein. Three months later, substantial Allied reinforcements enabled the new commander, Montgomery, to begin an offensive that secured North Africa.

7

7 The ruins of Monte Cassino monastery in Italy saw some of the most savage fighting of the war. The Allies believed that the Germans had turned the monastery into a strongpoint: their decision to bomb it not only provoked a controversy, it defeated its own end — the rubble was easier to defend than the intact monastery.

10

8

8 British paratroops experienced nine days of bitter street fighting – and final failure – at Arnhem in September 1944 when, with American and Polish forces, they attempted to capture 17 canal crossings and major bridges in Holland. Of the 35,000 troops involved, more than 17,000 became casualties. Four of the five major bridges were taken; the bridge at Arnhem was not. The plan devised by Montgomery – dashing, and contrary to his usual style – might have shortened the war had it worked.

9

9 Lieutenant-General William Joseph Slim (1891–1970) commanded the 14th British Army in Burma. In June 1944, he defeated a Japanese attempt to invade India at Kohima and Imphal, and then successfully went on to liberate the country.

10 The Japanese in New Guinea suffered their first major setback on land in September 1942 when Australian forces defeated an attempt to capture Port Moresby. After savage fighting in atrocious conditions, the Australians successfully counter-attacked. Throughout 1943 and early 1944, a series of small-scale but brilliant combined operations were mounted as part of a wider Allied offensive in the southwestern Pacific. These isolated and neutralized a whole Japanese army.

The Home Front in World War II

World War II has often, and accurately, been described as "The People's War". No previous conflict in history had so directly involved the civilian population of the combatant countries or caused them so much privation and death.

Civilian involvement in war

Even before war had been declared civilians had become involved through conscription, introduced in Germany in 1934, in Great Britain in June 1939, and in the United States on a selective "unlucky dip" basis in 1940. Once the war began even those civilians who escaped being called up into the armed forces found themselves in varying degrees directed into home defence (Local Defence Volunteers, later the Home Guard) [2] or civil defence or into essential work in factories [8] and vital services such as transport. In every combatant country (except the United States, which could meet almost all the demands made upon it) the share of the national resources allocated to civilians was by the end of the war sharply reduced to give priority to the fighting men.

Although they vastly outnumbered the soldiers, the civilians were in far less danger. Even in Germany casualties among civilians, including those caught up in military operations, were estimated at no more than 700,000 compared with 3,500,000 servicemen who died. The figures for Britain were 62,000 against 326,000 and for Japan 260,000 civilians compared with 1,200,000 servicemen; the United States had virtually no civilian casualties. But the civilian's life was far more at risk than in any previous war. Although each country claimed at first to be directing its bombers against only military objectives, such restraints were soon abandoned [11]. But bombs were not the main cause of civilian deaths. Under German occupation, far more deaths were caused by disease, famine and mass murder.

Civilian daily life

Even within occupied Europe daily life varied enormously between different countries. In Denmark, Hitler's "model protectorate", the standard of living was far higher than in Britain. In France, if one had access to the black market, it was also possible to live reasonably well. But in Holland by the winter of 1944–5 people were living on tulip bulbs and in the Channel Islands only the arrival of Red Cross parcels prevented starvation. All the occupied countries shared some shortages and discomforts. Fuel, both for heating and transport, was scarce [5]. Everyone's life was encompassed by curfews, permits and the fear of being rounded up as a suspect or forced-labour "volunteer".

In the countries still under arms the civilian population was encouraged to believe that a vast gulf separated them from their counterparts in enemy lands. Civilian experience in Germany probably had more in common with life in wartime Britain than in any other country. Both suffered the upheaval of evacuation [Key] and of long nights in shelters.

Almost all necessities were either rationed or hard to find and although the German system of control was more complicated and less efficient than the British there were many similarities between them. Household textiles and clothes, for example,

CONNECTIONS

See also
World War II: Britain's role
Britain since 1945: 1

In other volumes
Evolution of the Western democracies (29)
The twenties and the Depression (31)
East Asia 1919-45 (31)
World War II (31)
The Soviet Union since 1945 (31)

1 Saucepans were collected for aluminium for making aircraft after a British Government appeal in 1940.

2 Britain's Local Defence Volunteers were formed in May 1940. Here two railway men are briefed.

3 "Dig for Victory" was an early wartime slogan thought up to promote the campaign for home-grown food.

4 Air raids on London – the Blitz – began on 7 September, 1940, and lasted until mid-1941. In the opening phase the capital was bombed on 57 consecutive nights. In the first four months, 13,339 people were killed and 17,937 injured.

5 Refugees flooded on to the roads of Europe as the German armies advanced. This Frenchman's horsedrawn vehicle laden with goods was one way of overcoming the petrol shortage; bicycle taxis were also common.

6 Nazi military bands like this one, photographed in the Place de l'Opéra in Paris in June 1941, often played in public in the occupied countries. Ostensibly a goodwill gesture, they were also a symbol of German strength.

were rationed on a points system in Germany in 1940 and in 1941 the same system was used in Britain. To find consumer goods of any kind, from babies' prams to furniture, necessitated a long search and in both countries as coal was diverted to the war factories people struggled in winter to keep warm.

Food rationing made the deepest impact on most people and here, as in other spheres, the Germans probably suffered most. The same basic items were rationed in both countries: meat, butter, fats, bacon, cheese, sugar, jam, milk and eggs. But in Germany one also had to part with coupons for bread and potatoes, both plentiful in Britain [3], and there were no "lend lease" supplies from America to help fill empty stomachs.

American soldiers arriving in Europe readily admitted that "back home they don't know there's a war on". Even in the United States there was, in theory, some rationing – of many canned goods, sugar and coffee – but in practice there was no real shortage of any type of goods. The Japanese fuel shortage prevented their indulging in the constant ritual bathing demanded by tradition. Japan also suffered a near-breakdown in the railway and island-ferry transport systems, and by 1945 food supplies had shrunk to no more than 1,300 calories a day, less than half the normal minimum.

A new prosperity

If the war years brought unprecedented hardship to civilians they also brought many benefits. In both Germany and Britain, due to the fairer sharing out of food supplies and full employment, poorer families lived better than they had ever done before. Everywhere, rigid price controls kept the rise in prices within limits; by 1945 the cost of living was only a third higher than before the war.

For factory worker and farmer alike, in every combatant country, these were boom years. The new prosperity masked deeper long-term changes. The drift from country to city was accelerated; there was increased pressure for urban amenities to be extended to the countryside; it was demonstrated that full employment was not an impossible dream and everywhere people demanded a fairer social order after the war.

KEY

Evacuation was carried out by the British Government at the beginning of the war because of the fear of massive air-raids. Nearly 1,300,000 people, mainly children, left the cities.

7

7 War savings were encouraged by all countries to stop inflation. This US Victory Bond was designed by Walt Disney.

8

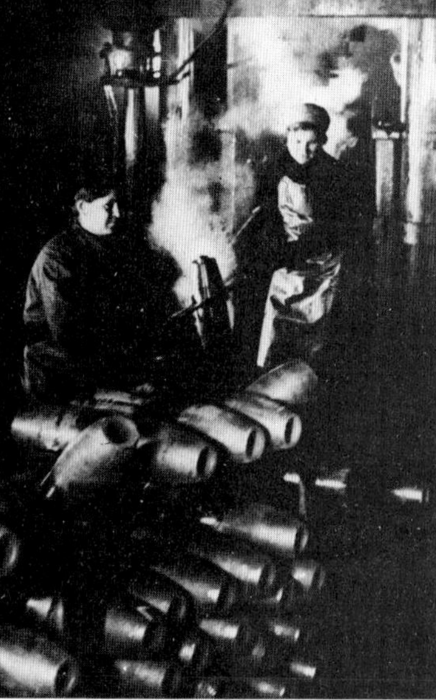

8 The mobilization of women was greatest in the USSR. Here ammunition is stacked to repel the Leningrad siege.

9

9 The destruction of Hiroshima on the morning of 6 August 1945 was the horrific culmination of the war in the Pacific.

10

10 Propaganda was used by both sides, both offensively and defensively. This German poster warns against careless talk.

11

11 Allied bombing devastated the non-military city of Dresden. These are the ruins of the church of St Sophia.

12

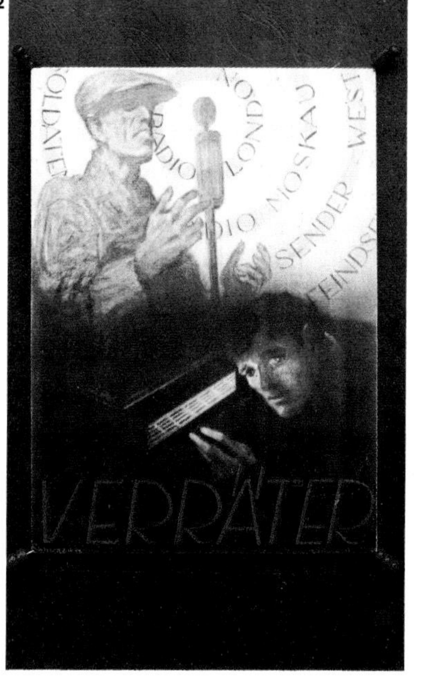

12 "Traitor" warns this German poster. German propaganda techniques were generally more sophisticated than the Allies'.

Britain since 1945: 1

After six years of war Britain's return to peacetime conditions needed a prolonged period of adjustment. Despite the remarkably united and disciplined war effort, the country's economy had been overstrained, and Britain was not in a position to shoulder properly the burdens of occupying its zone of Western Germany while also playing its part in achieving some kind of peace settlement in the East as well as in the West.

Labour victory and the Welfare State

Although Britain still ranked as one of the "Big Three" powers when the war ended, along with the United States and the Soviet Union, it soon became clear that it was no longer in the super-power league. At the 1945 general election, the bulk of the electorate showed that it was more interested in the approach to peacetime reconstruction offered by the Labour Party than in the continuation of Britain's role in big-power politics which it associated with Winston Churchill (1874–1965), linked as that would have been with a period of Conservative rule. A landslide victory for Labour deprived the country of the world figure who had been – not just for the British but for millions elsewhere – the personification of resistance to Nazism and Fascism. Clement Attlee (1883–1967) became prime minister.

Ernest Bevin (1881–1951) as Foreign Secretary supplied something of Churchill's bulldog quality in the negotiations that began to shape the peacetime settlement. At the same time he and others undertook the vast work of decolonization, starting with the granting of independence to India and Pakistan in 1947.

Domestic changes were almost as dramatic as those taking place outside Britain. The government's brand of socialism stressed nationalization of various sectors of the economy as the way forward, while greatly extending the state health and medical services and education, creating a "Welfare State" [4]. The Bank of England was nationalized in 1946 and in 1947 the railways and the coal mines were also taken under state control. The steel industry was also nationalized, in 1947, after a constitutional crisis brought on by Conservative opposition in the House of Lords, whose power to delay bills was subsequently reduced. What affected people most directly was the massive reorganization of the Health Services [2], accomplished by Aneurin Bevan (1897–1960), in order to provide medical and hospital treatment and prescriptions and also dental and other services "free", or at minimal rates.

The government had inherited a wartime economy. It continued rationing (not completely ended until 1954) and also policies of heavy taxation and wage restraint. Despite a large increase in exports, the country (or rather the sterling area as a whole) had an almost chronic deficit with the United States, which forced a devaluation of the pound from $4.03 to $2.80 in September 1949.

Conservative rule

Long-drawn-out opposition by the British Medical Association to the Health Service reforms, and bitter wrangling in Parliament over steel, indicated that Labour's popularity was waning. At the 1950 election Labour was returned to power with a reduced majority,

CONNECTIONS

See also
British foreign policy since 1919
Britain 1930-45
Britain since 1945: 2

In other volumes
The division of Europe (29)
Evolution of the Western democracies (29)
Europe from confrontation to glasnost (29)
Art and architecture in 20th century Britain (35)

1 A landslide victory brought Labour to power in 1945 with 393 seats against the 213 won by the Conservatives and their allies. The Conservatives and most foreign observers had assumed that Churchill, with his great wartime prestige, would carry them to victory. But the electorate was moved by Labour's promises of employment, housing and welfare and the proposals for nationalization of basic industries and state planning of the massive reconstruction that lay ahead. Years of wartime organization had left the people with a collectivist legacy that gave a strong appeal to Labour's socialist programme.

2 The centrepiece of the new Welfare State was the National Health Service, whose creation was the work of Aneurin Bevan. For the first time medical attention, prescriptions and many other services, generally became free or available on low charges. Some 3,000 hospitals were taken over under the scheme. While the hospital consultants welcomed the proposal, most of the doctors, organized by the British Medical Association, were bitterly opposed to it, as depicted in this contemporary cartoon. Bevan fought a long battle with the doctors, who saw in the scheme threats to their independence; but when the service began over 90 per cent of the doctors enrolled.

3 Rationing in the postwar period was more severe than in wartime. Until its defeat in 1951, the Labour government pursued an unpopular programme of austerity to rebuild the economy and finance government expenditure. Abroad things were serious; in The Netherlands and the British zone in Germany there was near famine and there was a lack of raw materials all over the world. But ironically a higher percentage of each age group in the London area in 1946 was classed as of "excellent nutrition" than in 1938, and this was true of the country as a whole. Rationing began to be reduced after 1948; in 1949 clothing and furniture were freed. Meat was the last item to disappear from the ration books, and that took place in 1954.

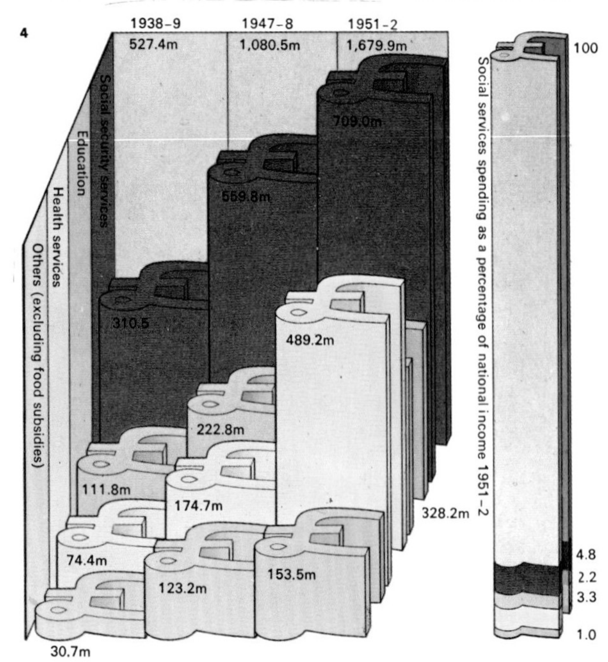

4 Figures for spending on the social services illustrate the economic reality behind the creation of the Welfare State. In 1938, the last full budgetary year before the war, social service spending was around £345 million or 37.6 per cent of total government expenditure; by 1950 this proportion had risen to 46.1 per cent. In 1955, R. A. Butler pointed out that during his period as Chancellor of the Exchequer, social service spending had increased by 40 per cent while the national income had increased by only 25 per cent. But government expenditure on defence remained high. The limited rearmament undertaken at the time of the Korean War (1950–53) deeply divided the Labour Party.

and at the following election in October 1951 the Conservatives under Churchill won a majority of 26. With this, they denationalized the steel industry in 1953 (it was renationalized by Labour in 1967).

The Chancellor of the Exchequer, R. A. Butler (1902-82), introduced measures to improve the balance of payments and to increase domestic consumption. The Conservatives were again returned to power in 1955 with an increased majority, with Anthony Eden (1897-1977) taking over as prime minister from the 80-year old Churchill, who resigned through ill health.

In domestic policies, Britain kept its independent nuclear deterrent [8] and continued national service (until 1958). Meanwhile, due in part to vast infusions of dollars through US loans and the Marshall Plan, the economy had a run of good years. The standard of living rose and the slogan "You've never had it so good" was coined by Harold Macmillan (1894-1986) [9], Conservative prime minister (1957-63) following Eden's resignation in the wake of the Suez Crisis.

Loss of confidence

In the early 1960s the economy took a downward turn and successive Conservative pay policies failed. Britain's application for membership of the European Economic Community (EEC) was vetoed by France in 1963, while the Beeching report proposing a one-third reduction in railway services also undermined Macmillan's popularity. Macmillan resigned because of illness in 1963 and was replaced by Sir Alec Douglas-Home (1903-) who could not restore confidence.

The general election of 1964 brought in the Labour Party and Harold Wilson [1], prime minister 1964-70 and 1974-6. Wilson tried to "save the pound" by large-scale borrowing from abroad, but lack of confidence in sterling led to its devaluation in November 1967. In 1973, under Edward Heath (1916-), Conservative prime minister 1970-74, Britain formally entered the EEC. Heath, however, could not improve the economy and, after failing to form a coalition in the election of February 1974, he was succeeded by Wilson in March 1974.

KEY

The Festival of Britain in 1951 was conceived as marking a new era of reconstruction following the destruction of World War II. Opened by George VI (*r.* 1936–52) on 3 May, it attracted 8.5 million visitors to the Festival Hall and other sights on the south bank of the River Thames.

5

...give him security and a proud future

THE CONSERVATIVE WAY

5 The 1950 election had returned Labour to power with a majority of only five. In 1951 under increasing pressure, the government resigned and an election gave the Conservative Party a majority of 26. The Conservatives presented an attractive alternative after the prolonged austerity of the preceding years.

6

6 The coronation of Queen Elizabeth II (1952–) in June 1953 was taken by many to symbolize a new "Elizabethan Age" with the promise of great prospects for Britain in the postwar world. The event was televised worldwide and thousands of cheering spectators lined the streets to watch the colourful procession.

7 A new youth culture emerged in the 1950s, alongside the beginnings of rock 'n' roll music, which presaged predominant youth cultures of the 1960s. Like the music, the new style was aggressive and uncompromisingly youthful and reflected the new affluence of the postwar period. Styles included those worn by "Teddy Boys", who affected Edwardian-style suits, string ties, and duck's-tail haircuts.

7

8

8 Ban-the-bomb demonstrations were frequent after the CND (Campaign for Nuclear Disarmament) was founded in 1958. Many public figures shared this widespread concern.

9

9 Harold Macmillan (left) was prime minister for six years from 1957–63 until he retired from the Conservative leadership because of ill health. During that time the country had a period of prosperous and efficient government, although the economic problems that dominated British politics in the 1960s became evident during the final years of his term of office.

Britain since 1945: 2

The 1970s found Britain in increasing economic difficulty. It failed to maintain its competitive position against trade rivals despite its entry in 1973 into the European Community (the "Common Market"), an entry that was reaffirmed after a referendum in 1975. Only through "invisible" trading (for example, banking, brokerage and insurance) did Britain keep its position.

Trade union militancy

Trade imbalances were offset by loans that became larger and larger. Trade weakness was caused by the higher productivity of competitors, and their greater ability to adopt new methods and machinery for both older industries and new, high technology enterprises. British management found it difficult to secure the co-operation of trade unions in introducing modern plants and reducing labour costs. This failure was coupled with successful union pressure for higher wages and fewer hours of work, backed by go-slows and strikes.

The Labour prime minister Harold Wilson (1916-) [1] in his two terms coped skilfully with the divisions in his party, but at the cost of compromising over important issues – to the point where governmental authority was eroded. At the same time the high costs of defence, education and the health service caused inflation to increase dramatically at times.

Edward Heath's (1916-) Conservative government (1970-74) fared no better in controlling inflation. An Industrial Relations Act established statutory wage and price controls, but crippling strikes, record trade deficits and the oil crisis could not be overcome. An overtime ban by the miners in the winter of 1973 led to a three-day working week to save fuel. When, in 1974, the National Union of Mineworkers called an all-out strike for higher wages, Heath sought a mandate for a firm line against union pressure. However, the general election brought in Labour with a majority of just five seats in Parliament; another election eight months later gave Labour a majority of 43 seats.

James Callaghan (1912-), who became Labour prime minister after Harold Wilson resigned, tried to curb inflation. He reintroduced an incomes policy, and supported the ailing giants of British industry with public funds. It was not enough, however, to stave off a "winter of discontent" in 1978-9. In May 1979 a Conservative government was returned to power under Britain's first woman prime minister, Margaret Thatcher (1925-) [8].

The era of Thatcherism

The priority of the new government was to reduce inflation by cutting public spending and discourage private borrowing by keeping interest rates high. This also meant a reliance on "free-market" forces.

There followed a sharp decline in Britain's manufacturing industries and a steep rise in unemployment [4]. In 1981, inner city tensions exploded in some cities, notably London (Brixton), Bristol and Liverpool. British victory in the Falklands War of April 1982 was followed by a huge Conservative election victory in 1983, ensuring a second term of office for Thatcher. In 1984, the miners began a bitter, year-long strike, but had to return to work

CONNECTIONS

See also
British foreign policy since 1919
Britain 1930-45
Britain since 1945: 1

In other volumes
Evolution of the Western democracies (29)
Europe from confrontation to glasnost (29)
Southern Africa since 1910 (31)
Art and architecture in 20th century Britain (35)

1

1 Harold Wilson (1916–) became prime minister of a Labour government with a majority of only four in 1964. He consolidated his party's position at a further election in 1966. The youngest MP to attain cabinet rank in the first post-war government (at the Board of Trade), he took over the party leadership after the death of Hugh Gaitskell in 1963. Although his flexibility enabled him to hold together the left and right wings of his party, his hopes of modernizing the British economy and the trade union system were dashed first by the weakness of sterling and secondly by union opposition to sweeping changes.

2

2 Holland Park Comprehensive made news as a large purpose-built (1958) school in a fashionable part of London to which some public figures sent their children. With its sixth form block, ten science laboratories, ten art studios, seven workshops and three gymnasiums, it summed up the aspirations of a new-style education system based on the principle of giving all children, no matter what their background or means, equal opportunity. As some academic standards slipped, however, Labour's policy of replacing grammar, secondary modern and grant-aided schools by comprehensives provoked increasingly fierce controversy.

3

3 Mick Jagger and the Rolling Stones, seen here at a 1969 concert in Hyde Park, London, were the most aggressive, irreverent, anti-establishment rock group to appear in the entertainment world of the 1960s. Their appeal was less broadly based than that of the Beatles, whose popularity with virtually all age groups helped to break down some of the traditional barriers of class and accent in Britain. The driving music of the Rolling Stones was directed more frankly at youthful rebellion. It chimed in with trends of the times, reflected in the increasingly open treatment of sex and violence in films and on television, and the use of drugs as stimulants on a scale previously unknown.

4

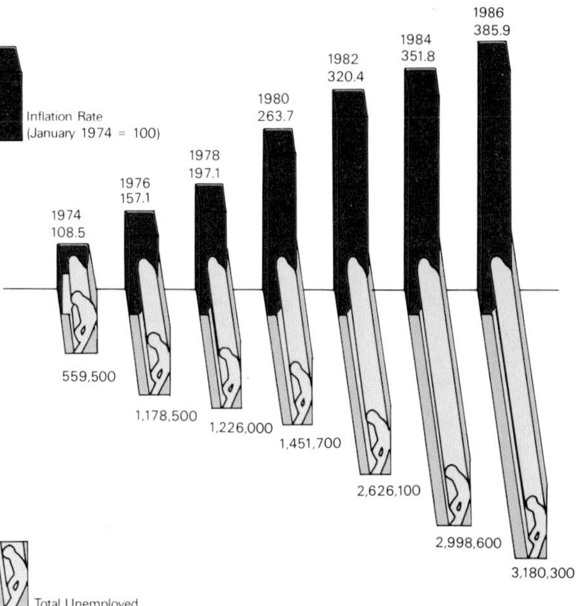

4 Inflation had risen at a rate of 3% to 4% from 1945 until 1964 as wage rises outstripped growth in production and government spending steadily increased. The rate jumped in 1967 as the 14.3% devaluation of the pound put up the price of imported goods. Soaring costs throughout the early 1970's, fuelled by oil price rises imposed by the OPEC nations, brought inflation to 20% in 1975 when the number of unemployed rose above 1 million for the first time since the 1930's. Inflation was brought under control in the 1980's although during this period the number of those out of work trebled. An alteration in the method of calculating the number of unemployed introduced in 1982, had the effect of reducing the official figure of those out of work.

with their demands unsatisfied [6]. April 1986 saw the abolition of the Greater London Council (GLC), which had governed the metropolitan area since 1965. Responsibility for the capital's services fell to various boroughs and authorities.

Privatizing industries

There was a decline in unemployment from the high levels of the mid-1980s, and the government was able to cut taxes significantly from the levels of previous administrations. In June 1987 Margaret Thatcher won her third successive election victory: the first British prime minister to do so since Lord Melbourne in the nineteenth century. Her third term was marked by privatization of public service industries (for example, gas and water), the introduction of a community charge ("poll tax") to replace domestic rates [Key], rising inflation and higher interest rates. By 1990, after 11 years in power, "Thatcherism" had begun to attract criticism for its autocratic style, while economic policies were resulting in discontent across the political spectrum.

After Labour's third election defeat the party, under its leader Neil Kinnock (1942-), radically reshaped itself to present a more moderate image to the electorate. Militant left-wingers were expelled, the policy of unilateral nuclear disarmament dropped, and a more pro-European stance adopted to counter the government's often near-isolationist stand on European issues.

The merging, in 1983, of the Liberal Party and Social Democratic Party (SDP) (formed by breakaway Labour MPs) gave rise to the Social and Liberal Democrats. The few who opposed the alliance kept their original SDP title and banded together under the party's co-founder, David Owen (1938-).

Beyond party politics, the 1980s revealed growing concern over the state of the environment. This awareness resulted in Britain's Green Party polling 15 per cent (over two million votes) in the 1989 elections to the European parliament. Among major environmental concerns were global warming (the "greenhouse effect"), the dumping of sludge and untreated sewage in the sea, and carbon dioxide emissions.

Protestors demonstrate their support for the campaign against the community charge or "poll tax" with a march in Edinburgh in April 1989. The community charge was designed to replace the system of domestic rates by taxing individuals instead of property. It was established in Scotland in 1989 and in the rest of the country in 1990.

5 Immigrants from the West Indies and Asia provided staff for medical, transport and postal services and for certain industries, notably textiles, after World War II. But their rising numbers and limited prospects brought social strains while problems of housing and education led to government measures to regulate their entry during the 1960s. The entry restrictions were partially waived to accommodate Asians holding British passports expelled from Uganda in 1972. Community services and immigration liaison offices were set up in several cities to help with their integration and improve race relations.

6 Striking miners in 1984 clash with the police at Kellingly, Yorkshire. The strike was against a 5.2% pay offer and a programme of pit closures, but as there was no national ballot, the strike was unofficial and many miners continued to work. This led to secondary picketing by militant strikers, resulting in violence and new laws against the so-called "flying pickets".

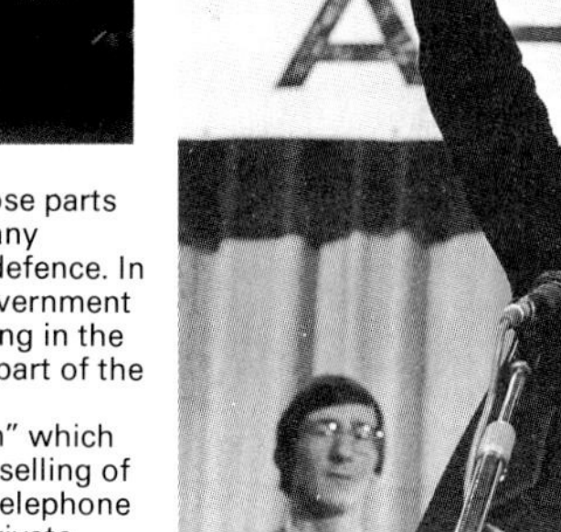

7 Rolls-Royce engine manufacture was threatened in 1971 when the company's financial problems forced it to seek assistance from a Conservative government pledged to leave "lame duck" industries to their fate. The government had to take over those parts of the company essential to defence. In 1987, the government sold its holding in the company as part of the policy of "privatization" which included the selling of the gas and telephone services to private shareholders.

8 Margaret Thatcher (1925-) was education minister in Edward Heath's government and replaced him as leader of the Conservative Party in 1975. She became prime minister after the Conservative election victory of 1979. During her time in office, the powers of trade unions and local authorities have been reduced.

9 The Falklands War in 1982 was the first occasion since the Suez crisis of 1956 that British troops were involved in armed conflict with a foreign nation. Argentinian troops landed on the Falklands Islands on 2nd April 1982 and on the 5th April a massive Task Force of British ships and troops set out for the South Atlantic. On June 14th, after a month of fighting in which 255 British servicemen died the Argentinians surrendered. A large garrison of British soldiers remained to defend the islands.

Index to Volume 28

Page numbers in *italic* refer to illustrations

The New Joy of Knowledge Encyclopedia
This updated and revised edition published by Oriole Publishing Ltd, Griffin House, 161 Hammersmith Road, London W6 8SD.

Printed in Spain by Printer Industria Grafica S.A.D.L.B. 26773-1989.

NOTE: Whilst every attempt is made to keep the price of volumes constant, the publishers reserve the right to increase the stated prices at any time when circumstances dictate.

Editorial Director
Eden Phillips

Editors
Stephen Fitzjohn
Belinda Weber

Sub-editor
Mike Brown

Editorial Assistants
Amanda Ball
Graham Coleman

Picture Research
Julian Jackson

Production Controller
Louise Flockhart

Advisers to the original edition
Dr. Robin Cormack
Professor Peter Lasko

PICTURE CREDITS
Cover, 1621 By gracious permission Her Majesty the Queen **1622-3** (Key) Weidenfeld & Nicholson Archives/British Museum (BM); (1) Michael Holford/BM; (2) Weidenfeld & Nicholson Archives (W&NA)/V & A. (3, 9) Mansell Collection (MC); (4, 5) Fotomas Index (FI); (6, 7) National Portrait Gallery (NPG); (8) Hulton Deutsch. **1624-5** (Key) FI; (1) FI/BM; (2, 4) Hulton-Deutsch; (3) Mary Evans Picture Library (MEPL); (5) Eileen Tweedy (ET)/ Museum of London (ML); (6) National Maritime Museum (NMM); (8) A F Kersting. **1626-7** (Key, 1, 7, 9) John F Freeman (2) Picturepoint; (3) Hulton-Deutsch; (4) FI; (5) Scottish NPG; (6) NPG; (8) Art Gallery and Museum, Glasgow; **1628-9** (Key) Aerofilms; (1, 2) FI; (3) Picturepoint; (5) Governor and Company of the Bank of England; (6) Hulton-Deutsch (7) ET; (8) Michael Holford; **1630-1** (Key, 3, 6, 8) MC; (1) Bridgeman Art Library; (2) Sun Alliance & London Insurance Group; (4) Hulton-Deutsch;(5) ET; (7, 9) FI. **1632-3** (Key) County Records Office, Bedford; (1, 3, 5, 6, 7) Museum of English Rural Life, University of Reading; (8) MC; (9) by Permission of the Earl of Leicester/John Webb. (Key, 8) National Gallery of Ireland; **1634-5** (1) Master and Fellows, Pembroke College, Cambridge; (2) Bridgeman Art Library; (3) C M Dixon; (4) Public Records Office of Northern Ireland; (5) FI; (6) Hulton-Deutsch; (9) MC; (10) ET; **1636-7** (Key) Scottish Tourist Board; (1, 7) MEPL; (2, 9) MC; (4) ET/BM; (5) Hulton-Deutsch; (6) MB Photograph; (8) Studio Swain, Glasgow/ Mitchell Library, Glasgow. **1638-9** (2,6) Ronan Picture Library; (5) A F Kersting; (7) Derby Borough Council and Art Gallery; (8) The Wedgewood Group; (9) Bridgeman Art Library/Lord Mountbatten. **1640-1** (Key) MC; (1, 2, 3) NPG; (4) ML; (5, 8) Hulton-Deutsch; (6) ET; (7) FI. **1642-3** (Key) Picturepoint; (1, 2, 7) Hulton-Deutsch; (4) Robert Harding Associates; (5) W&NA/NMM; (6) FI; (8) ET. **1644-5** (Key) FI/BM; (1, 2, 8, 9, 10) Hulton-Deutsch; (3, 5) FI; (4) NPG; (6) ET. **1646-7** (Key) W&NA/ National Monuments Record; (1, 3, 4, 5, 10) Hulton-Deutsch; (2, 8) NPG; (7) W&NA; (9) Aerofilms; **1648-9** (Key, 8) MC; (1) Punch Publications; (2) Robert Harding Associates; (3) Picturepoint; (4) J Bethell/National Trust/W&NA; (5) Geoff Goode; (7) NPG; (9) Bridgeman Art Library/The Guildhall Library and Art Gallery. **1650-1** (Key, 5, 6, 7, 8) Hulton-Deutsch; (2) FI; (4) MC; (9) Robert Harding Associates/ ML; **1652-3** (Key, 3, 5, 7) Hulton-Deutsch; (1) NPG; (4) Punch Publications; (6, 9) FI. **1654-5** (1) NPG; (4, 5, 7, 9) Hulton-Deutsch; (6, 8) MC. **1656-7** (Key, 8) Hulton-Deutsch; (2) MEPL; (5) Popperfoto; (7) NPG; (9) W&NA/ Labour Party Photo Library. **1658-9** (1, 3, 6, 7) ET/National Library of Wales; (2) Welsh Folk Museum/ National Museum of Wales; (5) Hulton-Deutsch; (8) NPG. **1660-1** (Key) NPG; (1) Giraudon; (2) MEPL; (3) Hulton-Deutsch; (4, 6) MC; (7) Punch Publications; (8) Popperfoto; (9) London School of Economics. **1662-3** (1) Imperial War Museum; (3) Heeresgeschichtliches Museum, Vienna; (5, 9) Image Press; (6) Chaz Bowyer; (7) Ullstein Bilderdienst. 1664-5 (1, 2, 9, 10) Hulton-Deutsch; (3) ET/WM The Camera Press; (5) Wilfred Owen Estate; (8) MC. **1666-7** (Key) London School of Economics; (1, 2, 3, 5, 6, 8) Hulton-Deutsch; (7) Syndication International. **1668-9** (Key, 1, 4, 5) Popperfoto; (2) Zefa; (3) NPG; (6) Gamma/ Liason/Frank Spooner; (7) Black Star; (8) Keystone; (9) Topham/AP (10) Camera Press. **1670-1** (Key) Popperfoto; (1, 2, 3, 5, 8, 9, 10) Hulton-Deutsch; (4) British Airways; (6) Graham Newell; (7) Butlins. **1672-3** (1) Documentation Francaise; (2, 3) Image Press; (4) Novosti; (5,9) Popperfoto; (6, 8) Imperial War Museum; (7) Official USAF photo; (10) Australian War Memorial; **1674-5** (Key, 1, 2) Hulton-Deutsch;(3) Imperial War Museum; (4) Fox Photos; (5, 6) Roger Viollet; (7) Angelo Hornak/Imperial war Museum; (8) Novosti; (9) Orion Press/Camera Press; (10, 12) Snark International; (11) IBA, Zurich. **1676-7** (Key, 1, 8) Popperfoto; (2) Punch Publications; (3, 7) Hulton-Deutsch; (5) Graham Nash/Conservative Party Archives; (6) Fox Photos; (9) Rex Features. **1678-9** (Key) Network/Lowe; (1, 3) Poppeerfoto; (2) David Strickland; (5, 8) Camera Press; (6) Impact/Sean Smith; (7) Rolls Royce Motors Ltd; (9) Picturepoint.